Vocabulary
AND
Composition

Through
Pleasurable
Reading

BOOK II

HAROLD LEVINE
Chairman Emeritus of English,
Benjamin Cardozo High School, New York

NORMAN LEVINE
Associate Professor of English,
City College of the City University of New York

ROBERT T. LEVINE
Professor of English,
North Carolina A & T State University

Vocabulary books by the authors

Vocabulary and Composition Through Pleasurable Reading, Books I–VI
Vocabulary for Enjoyment, Books I–III
Vocabulary for the High School Student, Books A, B
Vocabulary for the High School Student
Vocabulary for the College-Bound Student
The Joy of Vocabulary

Vocabulary
AND
Composition
Through
Pleasurable
Reading

BOOK II

When ordering this book please specify either R 554 W
or Vocabulary and Composition
Through Pleasurable Reading, Book II, Workbook

AMSCO SCHOOL PUBLICATIONS, INC.
315 Hudson Street / New York, NY 10013

Acknowledgments

Grateful acknowledgment is made to the following sources for having granted permission to reprint copyrighted materials.

HarperCollins Publishers. *Selection 10.* From OLD YELLER by Fred Gipson. Copyright © 1956 by Fred Gipson. Reprinted by permission of HarperCollins Publishers.

Houghton Mifflin Company. *Selection 5.* From THE HEART IS A LONELY HUNTER by Carson McCullers. Copyright 1940 by Carson McCullers. Copyright © 1967 renewed by Carson McCullers. Reprinted by permission of Houghton Mifflin Company.

Alfred A. Knopf, Inc. *Selection 4.* From LIFE WITH FATHER by Clarence Day. Copyright 1935 by Clarence Day and renewed 1963 by Mrs. Katherine B. Day. Reprinted by permission of Alfred A. Knopf, Inc.

McIntosh and Otis, Inc. *Selection 15.* From HOT ROD by Henry Gregor Felsen. Copyright © 1950, 1978 by Henry Gregor Felsen. Reprinted by permission of McIntosh and Otis, Inc.

Penguin USA. *Selection 8.* From THE PEARL by John Steinbeck. Copyright 1945 by John Steinbeck, © renewed 1973 by Elaine Steinbeck, Thom Steinbeck and John Steinbeck IV. Used by permission of Viking Penguin, a division of Penguin Books USA Inc.

Charles Scribner's Sons. *Selection 3.* Reprinted with permission of Charles Scribner's Sons, an imprint of Macmillan Publishing Company, from THE YEARLING by Marjorie Kinnan Rawlings. Copyright 1938 Marjorie Kinnan Rawlings; copyright renewed © 1966 Norton Baskin.

ISBN 0-87720-770-4

Printed in the United States of America

To the Student

Where did famous writers like Mark Twain, Robert Louis Stevenson, and Jack London learn their composition skills? To a large extent, from other famous writers—and you can do the same. In this book, you will not only be improving your vocabulary and critical reading skills, but you will also get valuable lessons in the art of writing from sixteen gifted authors, including Mark Twain (page 13), Robert Louis Stevenson (page 96), and Jack London (page 198).

Each unit in this book opens with an appealing passage from a well-known work, such as *The Adventures of Tom Sawyer, The Heart Is a Lonely Hunter, Treasure Island, The Pearl,* and *White Fang.* This opening passage is the inspiration for everything you will learn in the unit, not just about literature, vocabulary, composition, and reading, but also about how to think critically, and how to spell.

That, briefly, is our plan and purpose. Now, turn to page 1 for a sample of how rewarding and enjoyable it can be to use this book.

The Authors

For Your Reading Pleasure

UNIT III / Reading Selections 9–12

UNIT IV / Reading Selections 13–16

The Adventures of Tom Sawyer

by Mark Twain

On his way to school, Tom Sawyer meets Huckleberry Finn, son of the village drunkard. The respectable boys of the town have been forbidden to associate with Huck, but that makes them enjoy Huck's company all the more. Tom has a long conversation with Huck, and, as a result, he arrives at school late.

When Tom reached the little isolated frame schoolhouse, he strode in briskly, with the manner of one who had come with all honest speed. He hung his hat on a peg and flung himself into his seat with businesslike alacrity. The master, throned on high in
5 his great splint-bottom arm-chair, was dozing, lulled by the drowsy hum of study. The interruption roused him.

"Thomas Sawyer!"

Tom knew that when his name was pronounced in full, it meant trouble.

10 "Sir!"

"Come up here. Now, sir, why are you late again, as usual?"

Tom was about to take refuge in a lie, when he saw two long tails of yellow hair hanging down a back that he recognized by the electric sympathy of love; and by that form was *the only vacant*
15 *place* on the girls' side of the schoolhouse. He instantly said:

"I STOPPED TO TALK WITH HUCKLEBERRY FINN!" The master's pulse stood still, and he stared helplessly. The buzz of study ceased. The pupils wondered if this foolhardy boy had lost his mind. The master said:

20 "You—you did what?"

"Stopped to talk with Huckleberry Finn."

There was no mistaking the words.

1

"Thomas Sawyer, this is the most astounding confession I have ever listened to. No mere ferule will answer for this offense. Take
25 off your jacket."

The master's arm performed until it was tired and the stock of switches notably diminished. Then the order followed:

"Now, sir, go and sit with the *girls!* And let this be a warning to you."

30 The titter that rippled around the room appeared to abash the boy, but in reality that result was caused rather more by his worshipful awe of his unknown idol and the dread pleasure that lay in his high good fortune. He sat down upon the end of the pine bench and the girl hitched herself away from him with a toss of
35 her head. Nudges and winks and whispers traversed the room, but Tom sat still, with his arms upon the long, low desk before him, and seemed to study his book.

By and by attention ceased from him, and the accustomed school murmur rose upon the dull air once more. Presently the
40 boy began to steal furtive glances at the girl. She observed it, "made a mouth" at him and gave him the back of her head for the space of a minute. When she cautiously faced around again, a peach lay before her. She thrust it away. Tom gently put it back. She thrust it away again, but with less animosity. Tom patiently
45 returned it to its place. Then she let it remain. Tom scrawled on his slate, "Please take it—I got more."

Line 4. *alacrity:* liveliness
Line 24. *ferule:* ruler used in punishing children
Line 30. *abash:* embarrass
Line 40. *furtive:* secret

UNDERSTANDING THE SELECTION

Exercise 1.1: Close Reading

In the blank space, write the *letter* of the choice that best completes the statement or answers the question.

1. Tom tells the truth when asked to explain why he is late because he _____.

    (A) sees it is no use to lie
    (B) wants to make the girls feel sorry for him
    (C) wishes to entertain the class
    (D) wants to sit next to the yellow-haired girl

2. At no time in the selection does _____.

    (A) the master stop watching the pupils
    (B) Tom study his book
    (C) the class stop paying attention to Tom
    (D) the yellow-haired girl take her eyes off Tom

3. The selection suggests that _____ .

    (A) Tom has often been punished by the master
    (B) the pupils are absolutely quiet when they study
    (C) except for Tom, the behavior of the class is perfect
    (D) Tom is usually on time

4. Of all present, who LEAST suspects Tom's true purpose in telling the truth? _____

    (A) the master
    (B) the pupils on the boys' side
    (C) the yellow-haired girl
    (D) the other girls

5. The yellow-haired girl _____ .

    (A) pays no attention to Tom
    (B) shows some interest in Tom
    (C) hates Tom
    (D) asks to have her seat changed

6. Which of the following sounds is not heard in the schoolhouse in the incident reported in the selection? _____

    (A) murmuring
    (B) giggling
    (C) whispering
    (D) coughing

7. Which of the following statements is UNTRUE, according to the passage? _____

    (A) There are no chairs for the students.
    (B) The girls and boys sit on opposite sides of the classroom.
    (C) Only the master is addressed as "Sir."
    (D) The "unknown idol" (line 32) is the yellow-haired girl.

8. Of the following, which is the best title for the selection? _____

    (A) A Harsh Punishment
    (B) The Power of Love
    (C) Reading, Writing, and Arithmetic
    (D) An Astounding Confession

Going Over the Answers   To get the right answers to questions like the ones you were just asked, follow one simple rule: *never guess!* The proof for every right answer is in the selection. Do not put down any answer as correct unless you have found the proof for it in the selection.

    Here are the correct answers to the questions you have just done. Carefully note the reasoning used in arriving at these answers.

QUESTION 1:   *Why the Correct Answer Is D:*

The "electric sympathy of love" (line 14) attracts Tom to the yellow-haired girl. At the same time he notices that the only seat not taken on the girls' side is next to her. *Instantly,* he forms a plan and puts it into operation: he will *not* lie to escape punishment for being late. He will tell the truth about having been with Huck Finn because that will result in the punishment of being ordered to "go and sit with the girls." Nothing can please Tom more at this moment than the punishment of sitting next to the yellow-haired girl.

Why the Other Answers Are Wrong:

A. According to line 12, Tom is aware that lying can provide him with a *refuge,* or shelter, from punishment. Therefore, to lie might have been of some use to him.

B. Nothing in the selection shows that Tom gives any thought to the *girls.* The selection shows clearly that he is interested only in *one* girl.

C. The passage makes it clear that the reason for Tom's telling the truth is to sit near the yellow-haired girl. There is no indication that on this occasion Tom wishes to entertain the class.

QUESTION 2:   *Why the Correct Answer Is B:*

• Examine every reference to Tom and you will see that at no time did he study his book. At one point he pretended to study but was not really studying.

Why the Other Answers Are Wrong:

A. The master cannot watch the class while he is *dozing.*

C. After a while, the class stops paying attention to Tom and returns to the "accustomed school murmur" of studying.

D. The yellow-haired girl took her eyes off Tom when she "gave him the back of her head for the space of a minute."

QUESTION 3:   *Why the Correct Answer Is A:*

At least four statements in the selection suggest that Tom has often been punished by the master.

(1) "Tom knew that when his name was pronounced in full, it meant trouble."

(2) "Now, sir, why are you late again, as usual?"

(3) "Tom was about to take refuge in a lie" (probably, refuge from punishment by the master).

(4) "No mere ferule will answer for this offense." (This suggests that Tom has been hit with a ferule, or ruler, before for previous offenses.)

Why the Other Answers Are Wrong:

B. The selection suggests that the pupils are noisy when they study: "the drowsy hum of study" and "the accustomed school murmur."

C. The behavior of the class is not perfect. The pupils *titter,* and they exchange *nudges, winks,* and *whispers.*

D. Tom is usually late: "Now, sir, why are you late again, as usual?"

QUESTION 4:   *Why the Correct Answer Is A:*

If the master had suspected Tom's true purpose, he would not have sent Tom to sit next to the yellow-haired girl.

Why the Other Answers Are Wrong:

B. and D. Tom's classmates quickly see Tom's scheme, as shown by their "nudges and winks and whispers" and "the titter that rippled around the room."

C. The yellow-haired girl knows Tom is flirting with her because she "hitched herself away from him with a toss of her head . . . 'made a mouth' at him and gave him the back of her head."

QUESTION 5:   *Why the Correct Answer Is B:*

The yellow-haired girl shows interest in Tom. She watches Tom and observes that he is stealing glances at her. She gives him the back of her head, but only for "the space of a minute." She apparently will accept Tom's gift of a peach.

Why the Other Answers Are Wrong:

A. The selection shows that except for the space of a minute, when she gives Tom the back of her head, the yellow-haired girl pays complete attention to Tom.

C. It is a mistake to think that the yellow-haired girl *hates* Tom when she hitches herself away from him, or "makes a mouth," or gives him the back of her head, or at first refuses the peach. She does these things to flirt with Tom. She obviously *likes* him.

D. The yellow-haired girl does *not* ask to have her seat changed.

QUESTION 6:   *Why the Correct Answer Is D:*

There is no mention of coughing.

Why the Other Answers Are Wrong:

A. Line 39 proves that there is murmuring in the schoolhouse.
B. Line 30 shows that there is tittering (giggling).
C. Line 35 indicates that there is whispering.

QUESTION 7:   *Why the Correct Answer Is C:*

Not only the master, but Tom, too, is addressed as "Sir." See lines 10–11.

Why the Other Answers Are Wrong:

A. Lines 33–34 indicate that the students sit on benches, not chairs.
B. Line 15 shows that the boys and girls sit on opposite sides of the classroom.
D. Lines 12–14 reveal that the yellow-haired girl is Tom's idol.

QUESTION 8: *Why the Correct Answer Is B:*

The best title, as a rule, is the one that sums up more of the passage than any of the other suggested titles. Since *The Power of Love* explains what happens in lines 12–46 (more than three-fourths of the passage), and none of the other choices does nearly as much, we must select B as the best title.

Why the Other Answers Are Wrong:

A. *A Harsh Punishment* applies only to lines 24–29. The selection deals with much more than harsh punishment.

C. *Reading, Writing, and Arithmetic* cannot be supported as the best title. Reading and arithmetic are not even mentioned. The only reference to writing is the message Tom scrawls on his slate (lines 45–46).

D. *An Astounding Confession* is appropriate only for lines 16–24, a very small portion of the selection.

To sum up, to get the right answer:

1. Don't guess.
2. Find the proof for the right answer *in the selection.*
3. Check out the other answers to see why they are wrong. This will give you added proof that you have chosen the right answer.

LEARNING NEW WORDS

Line	Word	Meaning	Typical Use
44	**animosity** *(n.)* ˌan-ə-ˈmäs-ə-tē	ill will; resentment; hostility (*ant.* **good will**)	The old enemies have become friends. There is no longer any *animosity* between them.
23	**astounding** *(adj.)* ə-ˈstaund-iŋ	filled with bewildered wonder; astonishing; amazing; surprising	When Bud, who had never pitched before, struck out the first three batters, we couldn't believe our eyes. It was an *astounding* performance.
2	**briskly** *(adv.)* ˈbrisk-lē	in a *brisk* (lively) manner; quickly; energetically (*ant.* **sluggishly**)	The students who are slowest in coming to class usually leave *briskly* at the bell. The mountain stream flows *sluggishly* until the rainy season, when it becomes a raging torrent.

27	**diminish** *(v.)* də-'min-ish	become or make smaller in amount, size, or importance; lessen; decrease *(ant.* **increase***)*	At first my headache was unbearable, but after a while the pain *diminished*.
5	**doze** *(v.)* 'dōz	sleep lightly; be half asleep; nap	A slight noise will awake me if I am *dozing*, but not if I am sound asleep.
18	**foolhardy** *(adj.)* 'fül-,härd-ē	foolishly bold; rash; reckless *(ant.* **wary, cautious***)*	To go out in sub-zero cold without a coat is *foolhardy*. *Wary* drivers check traffic in all directions before changing lanes. Be *cautious*. The pavement is slippery.
32	**idol** *(n.)* 'īd-əl	one that is very greatly or excessively admired; worshiped	The students worshiped the tennis champion; she was their *idol*.
12	**refuge** *(n.)* 'ref-yüj	shelter or protection from danger or trouble	At the height of the storm we took *refuge* in the vestibule of a building.
30	**titter** *(n.)* 'tit-ər	half-suppressed laugh; nervous laugh; giggle	The face you made when your accuser wasn't looking was responsible for a number of *titters*.
14	**vacant** *(adj.)* 'vā-kənt	having no occupant; unoccupied; empty	On the bus trip home I had to stand, as there were no *vacant* seats.

APPLYING WHAT YOU HAVE LEARNED

Exercise 1.2: Sentence Completion

Which of the two choices correctly completes the sentence? Write the *letter* of your answer in the space provided.

1. The singer we are going to hear tonight is Barbara's idol. She owns _____ of his records.

A. none   B. every one

2. The apartment has been vacant since May 26, when the Browns moved _____.

A. out   B. in

3. Pete dozed in the theater because he ____.

   A. was very excited about the movie   B. had not had much sleep

4. After his defeat, George ____ to show that he had no animosity.

   A. left abruptly   B. shook hands with his opponent

5. ____ is foolhardy.

   A. Dashing across a superhighway   B. Seeking advice from others

6. It started as a titter, and quickly became a ____ laugh.

   A. half-suppressed   B. hearty

7. ____; you are walking too briskly.

   A. Try to catch up with me   B. I can't keep up with you

8. The ____ in recent months has greatly diminished our water resources.

   A. lack of rain   B. abundant rainfall

9. They offered to ____ home, but we were not in need of refuge.

   A. take us into their   B. come to our

10. The news that Melissa was to receive the math prize was astounding because she had never thought she ____.

   A. had a chance to win   B. was inferior to any of the other math students

Exercise 1.3: Definitions

Each expression below defines a word taught on pages 6–7. Enter that word in the space provided.

_____ **1.** in a lively manner

_____ **2.** person excessively admired

_____ **3.** sleep lightly

_____ **4.** ill will

_____ **5.** having no occupant

_____ **6.** foolishly bold

_____ **7.** become smaller in amount

_____ **8.** nervous laugh

_____ **9.** filled with bewildered wonder

_____ **10.** shelter from danger

Exercise 1.4: Synonyms and Antonyms

Fill the blanks in column A with the required synonyms or antonyms, selecting them from column B.

	Column A	Column B
_____	1. synonym for *unoccupied*	foolhardy
_____	2. synonym for *surprising*	animosity
_____	3. antonym for *wary*	titter
_____	4. synonym for *shelter*	astounding
_____	5. synonym for *nap*	idol
_____	6. antonym for *good will*	doze
_____	7. antonym for *increase*	briskly
_____	8. antonym for *sluggishly*	vacant
_____	9. synonym for *giggle*	diminish
_____	10. synonym for *worshiped person*	refuge

LEARNING SOME ROOTS AND DERIVATIVES

Suppose you have just learned that the adjective *vacant* means "unoccupied." Now, if you were to see the noun *vacancy* in a sign outside an apartment building, you could easily tell that it means an "unoccupied apartment." Also, if you were to come across the verb *vacate* (the residents were ordered to *vacate* the building), you would know that it means to "go away from," or "leave unoccupied."

A word like *vacancy* or *vacate* is called a **derivative** because it is derived (formed) from another word—the word *vacant*.

A word like *vacant* from which other words are derived is called a **root**.

Each word in bold type is a *root*. The words below it are its *derivatives*.

brisk *(adj.)*	Because of the heat the refreshment stand did a *brisk* business.
briskly *(adv.)*	Cold soda sold *briskly*.
briskness *(n.)*	The owner was obviously pleased with the *briskness* of soda sales.
doze *(v.)*	If you *doze* at your desk, it may be that you have not had enough sleep.
doze *(n.)*	A brief *doze* can be very refreshing.
dozer *(n.)*	Our conversation did not seem to disturb the *dozer* at the other end of the park bench.

foolhardy *(adj.)*	Since Tom is a poor swimmer, it was *foolhardy* for him to try to swim to the raft.
foolhardiness *(n.)*	As a result of his *foolhardiness,* Tom might have drowned.
idol *(n.)*	Which sports star, actor, or singer is your *idol*?
idolize *(v.)*	Which sports star, actor, or singer do you *idolize*?
refuge *(n.)*	People made homeless by the hurricane were given *refuge* in public buildings.
refugee *(n.)*	*Refugees* from the hurricane were given shelter in public buildings.
titter *(v.)*	Charley's comic expression made me *titter*.
titter *(n.)*	When Charley made a face, I could not suppress a *titter*.
vacate *(v.)*	Please notify us if some guests should *vacate* their rooms.
vacant *(adj.)*	Please notify us as soon as a room becomes *vacant*.
vacancy *(n.)*	Please notify us when there is a *vacancy*.

Exercise 1.5: Roots and Derivatives

Fill each blank below with the root or derivative just listed that best completes the sentence.

1. The ringing of the telephone awakened me from my _____.

2. A "no _____" sign outside the motel indicated that every room was taken.

3. Working with remarkable _____, the movers unloaded the van in much less time than I had thought it would take.

4. The _____, who has been given protection in our country, hopes to return to his native land once democracy is restored there.

5. We spoke in whispers for fear of awakening the weary _____.

6. The child cannot keep up with you if you walk at too _____ a pace.

7. The student telling the joke began to _____ long before the rest of the class saw anything to laugh at.

8. If you succeed you will become a hero, and people will _____ you.

9. The reckless youngster has just committed another act of _____.

10. During a fire drill, all students and teachers must _____ the building.

IMPROVING YOUR SPELLING: CONSONANTS OFTEN OMITTED

"Tom . . . saw two long tails of yellow hair hanging down a back that he recognized . . ."

One of the most difficult words to spell in the above quotation is *recognized*. Many students carelessly omit the **g** when they say the word.

The words below are similar to *recognized:* they each contain a consonant that is often carelessly omitted when the word is said or written. The troublesome consonant is highlighted; be sure to include it in your pronunciation and also in your spelling.

ArCtic	probaBly
canDidate	quanTity
FebRuary	represenTative
goverNment	suRprise
libRary	symPtom

Study the words just listed. When you feel you know how to spell them, do the exercises that follow.

Exercise 1.6: Word Completion

Insert the missing letters. Then write the complete word. The first question has been answered as a sample.

1. s _u_ _r_ prise   _surprise_

2. lib __ __ ry   _____

3. can __ __ date   _____

4. Feb __ __ ary   _____

5. sy __ __ tom   _____

6. rec __ __ nize   _____

7. gov __ __ __ ment   _____

8. prob __ __ ly   _____

9. repres __ __ __ __ tive   _____

10. quan __ __ ty   _____

11. Large quan __ __ t __ __ s of supplies are being

    delivered.   _____

12. The lib __ __ rian showed me how to use the card

    catalog.   _____

13. How many members are there in the House of
    — epresen — — tives?

    _____

14. The robbers wore masks to prevent rec — —-
    nition.

    _____

15. S — — prisingly, the horse that was supposed to
    come in last won the race.

    _____

16. Feb — — — — y 14 is Saint Valentine's Day.

    _____

17. As you know, the FBI is a gover — — ental
    agency.

    _____

18. You are prob — — — y right.

    _____

19. After an hour, the hikers began to show sy — —-
    t — ms of weariness.

    _____

20. The submarine sailed north into the A — — tic
    Ocean.

    _____

USING *IT'S* AND *ITS*

1. *It's* is a contraction meaning "it is."

> *It's* two o'clock.
> Jeff says *it's* raining.

2. On the other hand, *its* (no apostrophe) is a possessive meaning "belonging to it."

> The river overflowed *its* banks.
> The cat hurt *its* paw.

Exercise 1.7: *It's* or *Its?*

Insert *it's* or *its* as required by the sentence. *Hint:* If "it is" can replace *it's* and make sense, you can be sure *it's* is correct. Otherwise, use *its.*

1. Our team is proud of _____ record.

2. Don't remove the cake from the oven until _____ done.

3. _____ too bad you were not present.

4. You can't judge a book by _____ cover.

5. Sheila will take good care of the guitar because she knows _____ value.

6. Sometimes a dog disobeys _____ master.

7. Be careful with that knife; _____ very sharp.

8. Don't you think _____ time to go?

9. _____ not your fault.

10. The tornado destroyed everything in _____ path.

IMPROVING YOUR COMPOSITION SKILLS: AVOIDING REPETITION

There is a characteristic sound in Tom Sawyer's schoolhouse when the students are studying. Mark Twain refers to it three times in the brief passage on pages 1–2—each time in a different way. In lines 5–6 he calls it "the drowsy hum of study"; in line 17 "the buzz of study"; and in lines 38–39 "the accustomed school murmur."

Question: Why doesn't Mark Twain repeat "the drowsy hum of study" in lines 17 and 38–39?

Answer: He knows that such repetition would be uninteresting and boring.

Exercise 1.8: Using a Synonym for Variety

Make the writing below more interesting by replacing each boldfaced word with a suitable synonym. The first synonym has been entered as a sample.

1. I had thought that we might encounter some resentment, but I was wrong. There was absolutely no **resentment** toward us. __animosity_____

2. Since the car was totally wrecked, we are amazed that the driver was unhurt. What amazing luck! Wasn't it **amazing**? _____

3. The apartment that was unoccupied at the beginning of the year is still **unoccupied.** _____

4. Only a reckless person would dart between speeding cars when crossing a street. I hope you won't do anything so **reckless.** _____

5. The company's sales have been steadily decreasing. If they keep on **decreasing,** the company may go bankrupt. _____

6. In the event of a thunderstorm, about the worst place to take shelter is under a tree. Find a safer place of **shelter.** _____

7. He naps a great deal. We saw him napping only a short while ago. Look! There he is **napping** again. _____

8. They gave us a hostile look as we came in. Why are they hostile to us? We have no **hostility** toward them. _____

9. Now she looks fine and has plenty of energy. In fact, she moves so **energetically** that we have trouble keeping up with her. _____

10. Why do people worship him? His talents as a performer and his appearance are not outstanding. And yet, they **worship** him. _____

Up From Slavery

by Booker T. Washington

It is 1873, and you have just completed your freshman year in college. Everyone is returning home for the summer vacation—everyone except you. You can't go home because you have no money. What are you to do?

AT THE END of my first year at Hampton I was confronted with another difficulty. Most of the students went home to spend their vacation. I had no money with which to go home, but I had to go somewhere. In those days very few students were permitted to
5 remain at the school during vacation. It made me feel very sad and homesick to see the other students preparing to leave and starting for home. I not only had no money with which to go home, but I had none with which to go anywhere.

In some way, however, I had gotten hold of an extra, second-
10 hand coat which I thought was a pretty valuable coat. This I decided to sell, in order to get a little money for travelling expenses. I had a good deal of boyish pride, and I tried to hide, as far as I could, from the other students the fact that I had no money and nowhere to go. I made it known to a few people in the town
15 of Hampton that I had this coat to sell, and, after a good deal of persuading, one coloured man promised to come to my room to look the coat over and consider the matter of buying it. This cheered my drooping spirits considerably. Early the next morning my prospective customer appeared. After looking the garment over
20 carefully, he asked me how much I wanted for it. I told him I thought it was worth three dollars. He seemed to agree with me as to price, but remarked in the most matter-of-fact way: "I tell you what I will do; I will take the coat, and I will pay you five

cents, cash down, and pay you the rest of the money just as soon
25 as I can get it." It is not hard to imagine what my feelings were
at the time.

With this disappointment I gave up all hope of getting out of
the town of Hampton for my vacation work. I wanted very much
to go where I might secure work that would at least pay me enough
30 to purchase some much-needed clothing and other necessities. In
a few days practically all the students and teachers had left for
their homes, and this served to depress my spirits even more.

UNDERSTANDING THE SELECTION

Exercise 2.1: Close Reading

In the blank space, write the *letter* of the choice that best completes the statement or
answers the question.

1. Booker T. Washington _____.

   (A) has more than one problem
   (B) does not need clothes
   (C) is the only student who did not go home for the vacation
   (D) does not have a home to return to

2. Booker is inclined to _____.

   (A) seek help from his fellow students
   (B) blame others for his misfortune
   (C) keep his troubles to himself
   (D) complain to others about his hard luck

3. The selection _____.

   (A) describes how Booker acquired the second-hand coat
   (B) indicates that he sold the second-hand coat
   (C) fails to indicate whether he sold the second-hand coat or not
   (D) indicates that he did not sell the second-hand coat

4. As far as money is concerned, Booker seems to be in about the same situation as
   _____.

   (A) the customer for the second-hand coat
   (B) most of the other students
   (C) the teachers
   (D) the people in the town of Hampton

5. There is no evidence in the selection that Booker is _____.

   (A) homesick   (C) lonely
   (B) willing to work   (D) getting poor grades

6. In his attempt to sell the second-hand coat, Booker does NOT _____.

   (A) do any advertising
   (B) use persuasion
   (C) encounter obvious resistance to his asking price
   (D) permit inspection of the merchandise

7. What is the immediate cause of the problem that Booker is trying to solve in the selection? _____

   (A) his lack of money for traveling expenses
   (B) the end of his first year at Hampton
   (C) his failure to find employment
   (D) his disappointment over the overcoat transaction

8. Which of the following is the best title for the selection? _____

   (A) Going Home
   (B) The Art of Selling
   (C) Job Hunting
   (D) Vacation Problems

LEARNING NEW WORDS

Line	Word	Meaning	Typical Use
1	**confront** (v.) kən-'frənt	face, especially in challenge; meet face to face; oppose	Tonight the Mets oppose the Expos; tomorrow they *confront* the Giants.
18	**considerably** (adv.) kən-'sid-ər-əb-lē	greatly; much; to a large extent	There was hardly a scratch on our car, but the other vehicle was *considerably* damaged.
32	**depress** (v.) di-'pres	sadden; discourage; make gloomy (*ant.* **cheer**)	When you visit patients, try to cheer them up. Don't say anything that might *depress* them.
18	**drooping** (adj.) 'drüp-iŋ	hanging down; losing strength; becoming weak	After the storm, when the sun came out, the *drooping* flowers began to raise their heads.
19	**garment** (n.) 'gär-mənt	article of clothing	Dad saves his old *garments* so that he may wear them when he does messy jobs.

22	**matter-of-fact** *(adj.)* ‚mat-ər-ə-ʹfakt	sticking strictly to facts; unimaginative; concerned with the obvious and overlooking the deeper reality	The teacher showed me that my descriptions are too *matter-of-fact;* they lack imagination.
		*(ant. **imaginative**)*	A news story must stick to the facts; it should not be *imaginative.*
30	**necessity** *(n.)* ni-ʹses-ə-tē	very necessary thing; something that cannot be done without; need	Food, shelter, and clothing are *necessities*—everyone must have them.
31	**practically** *(adv.)* ʹprak-ti-kə-lē	almost; very nearly	We are going shopping, since there is *practically* no food left in the refrigerator.
12	**pride** *(n.)* ʹprīd	1. self-respect; sense of one's own worth or dignity	Sam has too much self-respect to back out. To be called a quitter would be a blow to his *pride.*
		2. delight or satisfaction in one's achievements or possessions	Grandma was pleased when I praised her pancakes. She takes *pride* in her cooking.
		*(ant. **shame**)*	
19	**prospective** *(adj.)* prə-ʹspek-tiv	likely to be or become; expected; probable	My brother introduced his *prospective* bride; they are to be married in June.

APPLYING WHAT YOU HAVE LEARNED

Exercise 2.2: Sentence Completion

Which of the two choices correctly completes the sentence? Write the *letter* of your answer in the space provided.

1. ＿＿ are not necessities.

    A. Jewelry and sports cars   B. Clean air and water

2. The news of your ＿＿ depressed us.

    A. unfortunate accident   B. safe arrival

3. We are looking ＿＿ our prospective vacation.

    A. back on   B. forward to

4. A _____ is not a garment.

    A. curtain   B. bathrobe

5. We returned to the field with the drooping spirits of a team that was sure to _____.

    A. win   B. lose

6. The new student arrived in _____, when the school year was practically over.

    A. May   B. November

7. Under our system of justice, a defendant has the right of confronting his _____.

    A. accusers   B. friends

8. Do you prefer a matter-of-fact news commentator, or one who _____?

    A. does not omit important details   B. looks into the deeper reality of things

9. When a student needs a scolding, Mrs. Kapp will give it to him in _____ to reduce the blow to his pride.

    A. front of the whole class   B. private

10. My brother is 21 and my sister is considerably younger; she is _____.

    A. 14   B. 18

Exercise 2.3: Definitions

Each expression below defines a word taught on pages 17–18. Enter that word in the space provided.

_____ **1.** sense of one's own worth

_____ **2.** article of clothing

_____ **3.** likely to be or become

_____ **4.** hanging down

_____ **5.** to a large extent

_____ **6.** make gloomy

_____ **7.** meet face to face

_____ **8.** sticking strictly to facts

_____ **9.** very nearly

_____ **10.** something that we cannot do without

Exercise 2.4: Synonyms and Antonyms

Fill the blanks with the required synonyms or antonyms, selecting them from the vocabulary list.

1. synonym for *almost:* _____
2. antonym for *imaginative:* _____
3. synonym for *clothing:* _____
4. synonym for *oppose:* _____
5. antonym for *shame:* _____
6. synonym for *need:* _____
7. synonym for *greatly:* _____
8. antonym for *cheer:* _____
9. synonym for *expected:* _____
10. synonym for *weakening:* _____

Vocabulary List

garments
depress
pride
prospective
practically
matter-of-fact
considerably
confront
drooping
necessity

LEARNING SOME ROOTS AND DERIVATIVES

Each word in bold type is a **root.** The words below it are its **derivatives.**

confront *(v.)*	My opponent has refused to take part in a debate because he is afraid to *confront* me.
confrontation *(n.)*	My opponent is seeking to avoid a *confrontation* with me.
considerable *(adj.)*	You have shown *considerable* improvement.
considerably *(adv.)*	You have improved *considerably.*
depress *(v.)*	Does losing *depress* you?
depressing *(adj.)*	To me, a loss is *depressing.*
depressingly *(adv.)*	My score was *depressingly* low.
depression *(n.)*	It threw me into a state of *depression.*
droop *(v.)*	Plants may *droop* from a lack of moisture.
drooping *(adj.)*	Rain gives *drooping* plants a new lease on life.
droopingly *(adv.)*	Thirsty plants bow their heads *droopingly.*
matter-of-fact *(adj.)*	The reporter wrote a *matter-of-fact* account of the event.
matter-of-factly *(adv.)*	She reported the event *matter-of-factly.*
matter-of-factness *(n.)*	She described the event with *matter-of-factness.*

necessity *(n.)*	Is a bicycle a *necessity* for the job?
necessary *(adj.)*	Will a bicycle be *necessary*?
necessarily *(adv.)*	Do you *necessarily* have to have a bicycle?
necessitate *(v.)*	Does the job *necessitate* that you have a bicycle?
prospect *(n.)*	The *prospect* of a snowfall appealed to the children.
prospective *(adj.)*	The children were happy about the *prospective* snowfall.
proud *(adj.)*	We are *proud* of our work.
proudly *(adv.)*	We talk *proudly* of our work.
pride *(n.)*	We speak of our work with *pride.*
pride *(v.)*	We *pride* ourselves on our work.

Exercise 2.5: Roots and Derivatives

Fill each blank with the root or derivative just listed that best completes the sentence.

1. You cannot learn a foreign language overnight. It takes a _____ amount of time and study.

2. The banners that had fluttered so proudly began to _____ in the dying breeze.

3. Our record this year of eight defeats and no victories is very _____. Most of the team is discouraged.

4. The opposing candidates have agreed to debate the issues face to face. Their first _____ will be on Channel 6 tomorrow at 10 P.M.

5. Here are two very urgent problems that _____ our immediate attention.

6. There is a strong likelihood that Stan will make a complete recovery, but there is little _____ that he will be able to play in any of the remaining games this season.

7. Poets write imaginatively, not _____.

8. Maureen, who is usually very cheerful, is in a state of _____ because she has not been invited to Alison's party.

9. Take along only what is _____ for the trip. Do not burden yourself with things you can do without.

10. My sister takes delight in her achievements as an honor pupil, while I _____ myself on being a good athlete.

A *compound word* is formed from two or more words joined together.

Note that a compound word usually *keeps all the letters of the words from which it is formed.*

some + one = someone
team + mate = teammate
none + the + less = nonetheless

Exercise 2.6: Writing Compound Words

A. Form three compound words with each italicized word. Study the two examples that follow.

door + step = **doorstep**   color + *less* = **colorless**
    + way = **doorway**   odor +   = **odorless**
    + knob = **doorknob**   taste +   = **tasteless**

1. *some* + body = _____   **2.** book + *keeper* = _____
      + one   = _____   house +   = _____
      + where = _____   store +   = _____

3. *home* + made = _____   **4.** class + *mate* = _____
      + less = _____   ship +   = _____
      + work = _____   room +   = _____

5. *no* + where = _____   **6.** sea   + *sick* = _____
     + body = _____   heart +   = _____
     + thing = _____   home +   = _____

7. *every* + one   = _____   **8.** head + *ache* = _____
       + thing = _____   back +   = _____
       + where = _____   tooth +   = _____

9. *any* + where = _____   **10.** road + *way* = _____
     + one   = _____   alley +   = _____
     + body = _____   drive +   = _____

B. Write the compound word.

    1. never + the + less = _____

    2. here + by   = _____

    3. dumb + bell   = _____

    4. extra + ordinary = _____

5. hair + do = _____

6. in + as + much = _____

7. up + keep = _____

8. hand + kerchief = _____

9. here + to + fore = _____

10. make + up = _____

Exercise 2.7: Proofreading

One word in each line is misspelled. Spell that word correctly in the space at the right.

1. timekeeper, somwhere, everyone _____

2. homemade, salesclerk, roomate _____

3. doornob, passageway, gentleman _____

4. painless, hankerchief, toothache _____

5. anyone, nowhere, somone _____

6. salesgirl, bookeeper, hereafter _____

7. teamate, seasick, heartless _____

8. penmanship, busineslike, shoeless _____

9. housekeeper, everyone, dumbell _____

10. heretofore, extrordinary, mailbag _____

AVOIDING DOUBLE NEGATIVES

QUESTION: He did not have _____ money. (*no* or *any*?)

ANSWER: He did not have *any* money.

EXPLANATION: In making a negative statement, we use only one negative word. Since the sentence already contains one negative word, *not*, it would be a mistake to choose *no*, which is also a negative word. Therefore *any* is the correct answer.

ALSO CORRECT: He had *no* money.

EXPLANATION: In this case *no* may be used, since the sentence contains no other negative word.

The following are some common negative words. Be careful to use only one of them in each negative statement:

no	never	no one	neither	scarcely
not	nobody	none	barely	only
-n't	nowhere	nothing	hardly	but (meaning *only*)

Exercise 2.8: Completing a Negative Sentence

One negative word is identified in each sentence below to warn you that you may not use another negative word in that sentence. Complete the sentence by writing the correct choice.

1. I didn't have _____ to do with it.
   (anything, nothing)

2. Sam has hardly _____ friends.
   (any, no)

3. Try to catch some worms; we couldn't find _____.
   (none, any)

4. Where are Joe and Bill? I have not seen _____ of them today.
   (either, neither)

5. Our teacher didn't fail _____ in that test.
   (nobody, anybody)

6. You did it yourself. You don't have _____ else to blame.
   (no one, anyone)

7. Jim's brother _____ barely five feet tall.
   (is, isn't)

8. Most of us haven't _____ gone camping.
   (never, ever)

9. I _____ but two sheets of paper left.
   (have, haven't)

10. She told us that she _____ nothing to do with Laura.
    (didn't have, had)

Exercise 2.9: Two Correct Ways to Make a Negative Statement

Below, on line A, is one correct way of making a negative statement. On line B, make the same statement in another equally correct way.

1. A. You have not answered any of my questions.
   B. **You have answered none of my questions.**

2. A. Don't mention it to anyone.
   B. **Mention it to no one.**

3. A. There are no napkins left.
   B. _____

4. A. I didn't care for either of them.
   B. _____

5. A. She had never been to the zoo.

   B. _____

6. A. They didn't have anybody to help them.

   B. _____

7. A. He has nothing to complain about.

   B. _____

8. A. I looked for errors but I found none.

   B. _____

9. A. We are not getting anywhere.

   B. _____

10. A. There aren't any signs of improvement.

   B. _____

IMPROVING YOUR COMPOSITION SKILLS: EXPLAINING A PROBLEM

Reread Booker T. Washington's first paragraph on page 15. Note that he organizes it as follows:

Sentence 1 states that he has a problem, or "difficulty."
Sentences 2–5 explain what the problem is.
Sentence 6 sums up the problem and ends the paragraph.

Exercise 2.10: Explaining a Problem
Using the above plan of organization, write a paragraph explaining a problem.

Hints for Topics: Choose either a personal problem or a community problem.

Personal: Finding a quiet place to study
             Watching too much TV
             Finding dependable friends

Community: Improving air quality
             Fighting crime
             Preventing drunken driving

Sample Paragraph: A Personal Problem

One of my chief problems is that I do not have a quiet place to study. Since we live in a small apartment, I must share a room with my brothers. Even when I am alone in the room and the door is closed, it is hard to concentrate. I am disturbed by sounds from the TV, or radio, or telephone conversations. I have become very unpopular with my family because I so often ask them to lower their voices. It would be much easier to do my schoolwork if I had a quiet place to study.

Note how the above paragraph is organized: Sentence 1 states a problem. Sentences 2–5 explain the problem. Sentence 6 sums up the problem and concludes the paragraph. The paragraph below is organized in the same way.

Sample Paragraph: A Community Problem

Air pollution is a serious problem in our area. We encounter it indoors, when people have been smoking, and outdoors, where motor vehicle exhaust pollutes the air. Scientists have warned for years that polluted air is a threat to our health. It seems these warnings are not being taken seriously enough. The fact is that air pollution is growing worse, especially in densely populated communities. We must therefore take immediate action to improve the quality of the air we breathe.

Now write your paragraph.

_____

_____

_____

_____

_____

_____

_____

_____

_____

The Yearling

by Marjorie Kinnan Rawlings

Jody Baxter, his father Penny, and their dogs Julia and Rip close in on Old Slewfoot, the huge black bear that has destroyed some of the Baxter livestock. Suddenly, Julia barks and Penny runs ahead, shouting.

"The Creek!" he shouted. "He's tryin' to make the Creek!"

Sound filled the swamp. Saplings crashed. The bear was a black hurricane, mowing down obstructions. The dogs barked and bayed. The roaring in Jody's ears was his heart pounding. A
5 bamboo vine tripped him and he sprawled and was on his feet again. Penny's short legs churned in front of him like paddles. Slewfoot would make Juniper Creek before the dogs could halt him at bay.

A clear space opened at the creek's bank. Jody saw a vast black
10 shapeless form break through. Penny halted and lifted his gun. On the instant, a small brown missile hurled itself at the shaggy head. Old Julia had caught up with her enemy. She leaped and retreated, and in the moment of retreat, was at him again. Rip darted in beside her. Slewfoot wheeled and slashed at him. Julia
15 flashed at his flank. Penny held his fire. He could not shoot, for the dogs.

Old Slewfoot was suddenly, deceptively, indifferent. He seemed to stand baffled, slow and uncertain, weaving back and forth. He whined, like a child whimpering. The dogs backed off an instant.
20 The moment was perfect for a shot and Penny swung his gun to his shoulder, drew a bead on the left cheek, and pulled the trigger. A harmless pop sounded. He cocked the hammer again and pulled the trigger once more. The sweat stood out on his forehead. Again

the hammer clicked futilely. Then a black storm broke. It roared
25 in on the dogs with incredible swiftness. White tusks and curved
claws were streaks of lightning across it. It snarled and whirled
and gnashed its teeth and slashed in every direction. The dogs
were as quick. Julia made swift sorties from the rear, and when
Slewfoot wheeled to rake at her, Rip leaped for the hairy throat.
30 Jody was in a paralysis of horror. He saw that his father had
cocked the hammer again and stood half-crouching, licking his
lips, fingering the trigger. Old Julia bored in at the bear's right
flank. He wheeled, not on her, but on the bulldog at his left. He
caught him sideways and sent him sprawling into the bushes.
35 Again Penny pulled the trigger. The explosion that followed had
a sizzling sound, and Penny fell backward. The gun had back-fired.
Rip returned to his attempts for the bear's throat and Julia
took up her worrying from the rear. The bear stood again at bay,
weaving. Jody ran to his father. Penny was already on his feet.
40 The right side of his face was black with powder. Slewfoot shook
free of Rip, whirled to Julia and caught her to his chest with his
cupped claws. She yelped sharply. Rip hurled himself at the back
and buried his teeth in the hide.
Jody screamed, "He's killin' Julia!"
45 Penny ran desperately into the heart of the fracas. He jammed
the gun barrel in the bear's ribs. Even in her pain, Julia had taken
a grip on the black throat above her. Slewfoot snarled and turned
suddenly and plunged down the bank of the creek and into the
deep water. Both dogs kept their hold. Slewfoot swam madly. Only
50 Julia's head showed above water, below the bear's snout. Rip rode
the broad back with bravado. Slewfoot made the far bank and
scrambled up its side. Julia loosed her hold and dropped limply on
the earth. The bear plunged toward the dense thicket. For a
moment more Rip stayed with him. Then, confused, he too dropped
55 away and turned back uncertainly to the creek. He snuffed at Julia
and sat down on his haunches and howled across the water. There
was a crashing in the distant undergrowth, then silence.

Line 4. *bayed:* howled

Line 8. *at bay:* with escape cut off

Line 28. *sorties:* attacks

Line 29. *rake:* scratch

Line 30. *paralysis:* loss of ability to act

Line 45. *fracas:* noisy fight

Line 51. *bravado:* show of bravery

Exercise 3.1: Close Reading

In the blank space, write the *letter* of the choice that best completes the statement or answers the question.

1. During the battle with Slewfoot, Jody _____.

   (A) pokes him in the ribs
   (B) pulls Old Julia to safety
   (C) screams
   (D) remains calm

2. In their attack on the bear, _____.

   (A) Old Julia leads and Rip follows
   (B) Rip leads and Old Julia follows
   (C) the dogs do not work together as a team
   (D) the dogs give Penny no chance for a shot

3. When a gun barrel is jammed into his ribs, Slewfoot _____.

   (A) yelps in pain
   (B) plunges into the creek
   (C) shakes himself free of the dogs
   (D) stands baffled

4. The most seriously injured in this fierce encounter was _____.

   (A) Penny
   (B) Old Slewfoot
   (C) Rip
   (D) Old Julia

5. The bear escapes mainly because of _____.

   (A) his cleverness
   (B) Penny's poor marksmanship
   (C) the dogs' cowardice
   (D) equipment failure

6. The main target of the attacking dogs was Old Slewfoot's _____.

   (A) right flank
   (B) throat
   (C) head
   (D) back

7. In lines _____, the author expresses some sympathy for the bear.

    (A) 2–3
    (B) 9–10
    (C) 18–19
    (D) 40–43

8. Which of the following is the best title for the selection? _____

    (A) Cries in the Wilderness
    (B) A Water Struggle
    (C) Scars of Battle
    (D) A Vain Pursuit

LEARNING NEW WORDS

Line	Word	Meaning	Typical Use
18	**baffle** (*v.*) baf-əl	confuse, so as to keep from understanding; puzzle; perplex	At first I didn't recognize you. Your clever disguise *baffled* me.
17	**deceptively** (*adv.*) di-'sep-tiv-lē	in a *deceptive* (misleading) way; trickily	As the unsuspecting intruder walked into the ambush, all was *deceptively* quiet and peaceful.
		(*ant.* **genuinely**)	When I asked for permission to go home, I was *genuinely* ill. I was not pretending.
53	**dense** (*adj.*) 'dens	1. packed tightly together; compact; thick	The thief escaped capture by mingling with the *dense* crowd.
		(*ant.* **sparse**)	An overflow crowd had been expected, but the turnout was *sparse*.
		2. mentally dull; slow to understand; stupid	Three of my friends have explained the first problem to me, but I still don't understand it. I fear I am becoming *dense*.
		(*ant.* **bright, intelligent**)	
15	**flank** (*n.*) 'flaŋk	fleshy side between the ribs and the hip; right or left side of a formation; side	The cow kept swishing her tail to chase the flies from her *flank*.

24	**futilely** *(adv.)* 'fyü-ˌtəl-ē	in a *futile* (vain) manner; vainly; uselessly	My sister raised her fist *futilely* at the waves that were knocking her down.
		(ant. **effectively**)	We tried to stop the leak without success; however, the plumber dealt with it *effectively*.
25	**incredible** *(adj.)* in-'kred-ə-bəl	too extraordinary to be believed; hard to believe; unbelievable	Light travels at the *incredible* speed of 186,000 miles a second.
		(ant. **believable, credible**)	When a report comes from a *credible* source, we are inclined to accept it without question.
17	**indifferent** *(adj.)* in-'dif-rənt	showing no concern, interest, or feeling; uninterested; unconcerned	Most students are concerned about whether they will pass or fail, but Ed seems *indifferent*.
		(ant. **eager**)	
11	**missile** *(n.)* 'mis-əl	weapon or object thrown at a target; projectile	In her anger, Mary threw a shoe at me because it was the nearest thing she could use as a *missile*.
3	**obstruction** *(n.)* äb-'strək-shən	something that *obstructs* or is in the way; hindrance; obstacle	A disabled vehicle in the middle of a road is an *obstruction* to traffic.
11	**shaggy** *(adj.)* 'shag-ē	covered with a thick, rough mass of hair; hairy	Dad took the twins to the barber because they were beginning to look *shaggy*.

APPLYING WHAT YOU HAVE LEARNED

Exercise 3.2: Sentence Completion

Which of the two choices correctly completes the sentence? Write the *letter* of your answer in the space provided.

1. A _____ can easily be used as a missile.

A. stone

B. highway

2. With opponents swiftly closing in on the flanks, I had nowhere to run but ____ .

    A. to the right   B. straight ahead

3. Shaggy dogs have ____ coats of fur.

    A. thick   B. thin

4. It is not easy to ____ in the dense woods.

    A. hide   B. see ahead

5. Joe's explanation was incredible; ____ believed it.

    A. no one   B. everyone

6. The bundle was deceptively heavy; it seemed to be ____ to lift.

    A. hard   B. easy

7. The youngster screamed futilely; ____ .

    A. his parents came running   B. no one paid attention

8. An indifferent person has ____ for those who suffer.

    A. no concern   B. great pity

9. The crossword puzzle in the school newspaper baffled me. I ____ .

    A. did it in about a quarter of an hour   B. haven't been able to finish it

10. An obstruction ____ .

    A. blocks passage   B. prevents delay

Exercise 3.3: Definitions

Each expression below defines a word taught on pages 30–31. Enter that word in the space provided.

_____   **1.** too extraordinary to be believed

_____   **2.** packed tightly together

_____   **3.** something in the way

_____   **4.** showing no concern

_____   **5.** in a misleading way

_____   **6.** weapon thrown at a target

_____   **7.** covered with a mass of hair

_____   **8.** fleshy side between ribs and hip

_____   **9.** in a vain manner

_____   **10.** confuse, so as to keep from understanding

Exercise 3.4: Synonyms and Antonyms

A. Replace the italicized word with a *synonym* from the vocabulary list below.

_____ 1. The parade proceeded in an orderly manner with mounted policemen on each *side* of the marchers.

_____ 2. A *projectile* was thrown by someone in the crowd, but it landed harmlessly.

_____ 3. My brother's heavy dark beard and sideburns gave him a *hairy* appearance.

_____ 4. Vague language is a serious *hindrance* to communication.

_____ 5. These directions are very clear and should not *perplex* anybody.

B. Replace each italicized word with an *antonym* from the vocabulary list.

_____ 6. The goods were on sale at *genuinely* reduced prices.

_____ 7. The report seemed *believable*.

_____ 8. Because of the weather, the crowds at the beaches were *sparse*.

_____ 9. When I spoke to Nina about joining our club, she seemed *eager*.

_____ 10. Some consumers have protested *effectively* against higher food costs.

Vocabulary List

shaggy	indifferent
incredible	flank
futilely	baffle
missile	dense
deceptively	obstruction

Each word in bold type below is a **root**. The words below it are its **derivatives**.

baffle *(v.)*	How do you solve that problem? It *baffles* me.
baffling *(adj.)*	I find that problem very *baffling*.
deceive *(v.)*	Do you think I will *deceive* you?
deceptive *(adj.)*	I am not *deceptive*. I tell the truth.
deceptively *(adv.)*	I do not behave *deceptively*.
deception *(n.)*	I do not practice *deception*.
deceiver *(n.)*	I am no *deceiver*.
dense *(adj.)*	Some cities have a *dense* population.
densely *(adv.)*	Farm areas are not *densely* populated.
density *(n.)*	Farm areas have a low population *density*.
flank *(n.)*	Our ball-carrier needs protection on his right *flank*.
flank *(v.)*	I will *flank* him on the right if you will protect him on the left side.
futile *(adj.)*	Our opponents were too husky. It was *futile* to try to stop them.
futilely *(adv.)*	We tried *futilely* to stop our opponents; they kept scoring.
futility *(n.)*	Despite the *futility* of our efforts, we kept trying.
incredible *(adj.)*	You saved the game with an *incredible* catch.
incredibly *(adv.)*	You made an *incredibly* difficult catch against the right-field wall.
incredibility *(n.)*	We are still marveling at the *incredibility* of that catch.
indifferent *(adj.)*	I went to their assistance because I could not remain *indifferent;* they needed help.
indifferently *(adv.)*	When I saw they were in trouble, I could not pass by *indifferently*.
indifference *(n.)*	The two dazed travelers were standing beside their wrecked car. I could not look on with *indifference*.
obstruct *(v.)*	Sometimes legislators try to *obstruct* the passage of a bill.
obstructive *(adj.)*	They hold up passage of the bill by means of long *obstructive* speeches. Such speeches are called a filibuster.
obstruction *(n.)*	A filibuster is an *obstruction* to the passage of legislation.

Exercise 3.5: Roots and Derivatives

Fill each blank below with the root or derivative just listed that best completes the sentence.

1. We have laws that are designed to protect us from being misled by
   _____ advertising.

2. When the surrounded burglar realized that it was _____ to resist,
   he surrendered to the police.

3. As night fell, the _____ of the fog increased.

4. If you put hindrances in our path, you are being _____ .

5. It was a(n) _____ case, but Sherlock Holmes solved it.

6. Our farm areas are now sparsely inhabited, while our cities are becoming more
   _____ populated.

7. Myths, fairy tales, and legends appeal to us in spite of their _____ .

8. Marty has a strange _____ to the examination: he doesn't care
   whether he passes or fails.

9. You can depend on Josefina to tell the truth; she will not _____ you.

10. The disabled truck was towed off the bridge because it was a(n) _____
    to traffic.

Exercise 3.6: Defining Roots and Derivatives

Enter the word from page 34 that matches the definition below.

1. in an unconcerned manner	_____
2. ineffectiveness	_____
3. unbelievably	_____
4. be at the side of	_____
5. trickily	_____
6. perplex	_____
7. one who misleads	_____
8. stupid	_____
9. hinder	_____
10. trickery	_____

The black bear "snarled and whirled and *gnashed* its teeth . . ."

Notice that the **g** in *gnashed* is not pronounced. It is a silent letter, like the **t** in *listen*, or the **k** in *knee*.

Say each of the following words aloud, leaving out the silent letters. Remember, however, to *put the silent letters in when you write these words:*

SILENT *b*	SILENT *c*	SILENT *d*
bom*b*	des*c*end	han*d*kerchief
clim*b*	fas*c*inate	a*d*jective
com*b*	mus*c*le	a*d*join
crum*b*	s*c*issors	a*d*just
de*b*t	a*c*quire	(and all other
dou*b*t	a*c*quaint	*adj* words)
dum*b*	(and all other	
plum*b*er	*acq* words)	

SILENT *g*	SILENT *h*	SILENT *k*
desi*g*n	ex*h*aust	ac*k*nowledge
*g*nash	ex*h*ibit	*k*nack
*g*naw	g*h*ost	*k*nee
*g*nome	*h*eir	*k*nob
si*g*n	*h*erb	(and all other
	shep*h*erd	*kn* words)
	ve*h*icle	

SILENT *l*	SILENT *n*	SILENT *p*
a*l*mond	autum*n*	em*p*ty
ca*l*m	colum*n*	*p*neumonia
fo*l*k	condem*n*	*p*sychology
pa*l*m	hym*n*	recei*p*t
sa*l*mon		
yo*l*k		

SILENT *s*	SILENT *t*	SILENT *w*
ai*s*le	bankrup*t*cy	ans*w*er
i*s*land	Chris*t*mas	play*w*right
i*s*le	lis*t*en	s*w*ord
	mor*t*gage	*w*hole
	sof*t*en	*w*rap
	wres*t*le (the *w* is	(and all other
	silent, too)	*wr* words)

Exercise 3.7: Proofreading for Spelling

One word in each line below is misspelled; write that word correctly in the blank space.

_____ 1. unknown, climber, ajoin, plumber

_____ 2. adjusted, exausted, folk, descended

_____ 3. almond, fasinating, doubtful, bombshell

_____ 4. hym, wrestler, salmon, acknowledge

_____ 5. whole, knee, condem, isle

_____ 6. ghost, herb, knack, aquired

_____ 7. scissors, crumb, receit, bankruptcy

_____ 8. aquainted, dumb, knuckle, Christmas

_____ 9. yolk, neumonia, writer, column

_____ 10. playright, palm, muscle, shepherd

_____ 11. almond, wrist, anser, knee

_____ 12. calm, neebending, indebted, island

_____ 13. lissen, designer, bomb, heir

_____ 14. wrapping, exibition, knock, plumbing

_____ 15. combed, soften, morgage, vehicle

_____ 16. sword, adjoining, autumn, hankerchief

_____ 17. sychological, gnashed, doubtless, acquaintance

_____ 18. debtor, emty-handed, adjustment, dumbfounded

_____ 19. doornob, fascination, typewriter, folklore

_____ 20. aisle, column, adjacent, holeheartedly

Exercise 3.8: Writing Words With Silent Letters

One word in each sentence below has been omitted, but its pronunciation is given. You can tell the number of letters in the missing word by the number of spaces provided at the right. Study the following sample. Then fill in the other missing words.

I am in ['det] to my brother because I still owe him two dollars.

<u>d</u> <u>e</u> <u>b</u> <u>t</u>

1. Why don't you ['an-sər] her question? — — — — — —

2. It is impolite to ['kōm] your hair in public. — — — —

3. Do you prefer spring or ['ȯt-əm]? — — — — — —

4. A bicycle is a two-wheeled ['vē-ˌik-əl]. — — — — — — —

5. What do you have in the ['päm] of your hand? — — — —

6. Please keep your feet under your desk; do not put them out
   in the ['īl].   _ _ _ _

7. In the phrase "a wonderful time," "wonderful" is an
   ['aj-ik-tiv].   _ _ _ _ _ _ _ _ _

8. Do you want me to help you ['rap] the presents?   _ _ _ _

9. I tried my best, but I could not untie the ['nät].   _ _ _ _

10. The car would not start because the gas tank was ['em-tē].   _ _ _ _ _

USING POSSESSIVE PRONOUNS

In describing the bear, the author wrote:

"It snarled and whirled and gnashed its teeth . . ."

The word **its,** meaning "belonging to it," is the possessive form of the pronoun **it.**

A. Learn these **possessive pronouns** and their use:

POSSESSIVE PRONOUN	MEANING	USE
my and *mine*	(belonging to me)	It is *my* fault. The fault is *mine.*
your and *yours*	(belonging to you)	Is this *your* jacket? Is this jacket *yours*?
his	(belonging to him)	Johnny lost *his* key. Is this key *his*?
her and *hers*	(belonging to her)	This is *her* pen. This is *hers.*
its	(belonging to it)	A bird left *its* nest.
our and *ours*	(belonging to us)	Are these *our* tickets? Are these tickets *ours*?
their and *theirs*	(belonging to them)	Give them *their* share. Give them *theirs.*

You can see from the list above that NO APOSTROPHE is used with a possessive pronoun. Pay special attention to those ending in **s.** Like all other possessive pronouns, they are never written with an apostrophe.

RIGHT	*WRONG*
yours	your's
hers	her's
ours	our's
theirs	their's

B. On the other hand, a *possessive noun* DOES HAVE an apostrophe: the *boy's* ticket, the *girl's* share, etc.

Note again the use of the apostrophe in a possessive noun, but not in a possessive pronoun.

> These notes are *Mary's.* (possessive *noun;* apostrophe)
> These notes are *hers.* (possessive *pronoun;* no apostrophe)

C. Finally, do not confuse a possessive pronoun with a **contraction.** A contraction has an apostrophe, but a possessive pronoun—as stated before—does not.

APOSTROPHE OR NO APOSTROPHE?

apostrophe required:
> My **brother's** friend is a good tennis player. (possessive noun)
> Do you know where **they're** going? (contraction)

no apostrophe:
> **Ours** is the stronger team. (possessive pronoun)

Exercise 3.9: Using Possessives and Contractions

In the blank space, write the choice that makes the sentence correct.

1. The players took _____ places on the field. (*they're* or *their*?)

2. Let us know when _____ ready to leave. (*you're* or *your*?)

3. The owner of the jewel did not know _____ true value. (*its* or *it's*?)

4. Is the umbrella _____? (*her's* or *hers*?)

5. These are my keys. Where are _____? (*your's* or *yours*?)

6. Have you met my _____ husband? (*sisters* or *sister's*?)

7. _____ too bad you are ill. (*Its* or *It's*?)

8. Since our car is too small for all of us, let's ride in _____. (*yours* or *your's*?)

9. _____ is the second seat in the next row. (*Her's* or *Hers*?)

10. These sneakers must be _____. (*Tom's* or *Toms*?)

11. Do you know _____ parts? (*you're* or *your*?)

12. _____ a good chance of rain for tomorrow. (*Theirs* or *There's*?)

13. When the painter is done at your house, he will come to _____. (*ours* or *our's*?)

14. _____ was the better of the two talks. (*Your's* or *Yours*?)

15. Why won't you admit that _____ right? (*their* or *they're*?)

IMPROVING YOUR COMPOSITION SKILLS: VARYING THE LENGTH OF SENTENCES

Note the length of the following eight sentences in the paragraph by Marjorie Kinnan Rawlings (page 27):

1. Sound filled the swamp. (4 words)
2. Saplings crashed. (2 words)
3. The bear was a black hurricane, mowing down obstructions. (9 words)
4. The dogs barked and bayed. (5 words)
5. The roaring in Jody's ears was his heart pounding. (9 words)
6. A bamboo vine tripped him and he sprawled and was on his feet again. (14 words)
7. Penny's short legs churned in front of him like paddles. (10 words)
8. Slewfoot would make Juniper Creek before the dogs could halt him at bay. (13 words)

Question: The first, second, and fourth sentences above are very short. Why didn't the author make the other sentences in the paragraph short, too?

Answer: A paragraph of only short sentences would be choppy and monotonous. Varying the length of the sentences helps to make a paragraph more interesting.

Consider this paragraph:

> **It grew dark. A few drops fell. Gusts swept the streets. The temperature dropped. Pedestrians ran for cover. Lightning flashed. Thunder rumbled. Then it poured.**

Analysis: The above paragraph starts interestingly, but, as we read on, it becomes monotonous because all the sentences are of about the same length. However, see how the paragraph reads when we combine a few of the short sentences into longer ones:

> **It grew dark. A few drops fell. As gusts swept the streets and the temperature dropped, pedestrians ran for cover. Lightning flashed and thunder rumbled. Then it poured.**

Analysis: There is now greater variety in sentence length. The choppiness and monotony have been eliminated.

Exercise 3.10: Varying Sentence Length

In the space provided below, rewrite the following paragraph, introducing some variety in sentence length.

> **I rang several times. No one answered. I knocked. I shouted, "Is anyone home?" My words reechoed. There was no other sound. It was getting dark. I decided to leave.**

_____

_____

_____

_____

_____

_____

_____

_____

Life With Father

by Clarence Day

When your parents have a quarrel, who usually wins, Mother or Father? Why?

One day while Father was in his office downtown, Auntie Gussie and Cousin Flossie arrived. Mother immediately began planning to take them to dine at the Waldorf, a much-talked-of new hotel at Fifth Avenue and Thirty-third Street, which she very
5   much wanted to see. She knew Father mightn't like the idea, but he would enjoy himself after he got there, and she thought she could manage him.

When he came in, she went to his bedroom to break the good news to him that instead of dining at home he was to go off on a
10 gay little party. She meant to do this diplomatically. But she wasn't an adept at coaxing or inveigling a man, and even if she had been, Father was not at all easy to coax. Whenever she was planning to manage him, the very tone of her voice put him on guard; it had an impatient note, as though really the only plan
15 she could think of was to wish he was manageable. So on this occasion, when she tried to get him in a good mood, he promptly got in a bad one. He looked suspiciously at Mother and said, "I don't feel well."

"You need a little change," Mother said. "That'll make you
20 feel better. Besides, Gussie's here and she wants to dine with us tonight at the Waldorf."

Father hated surprise attacks of this kind. No matter how placid he might be, he instantly got hot when one came. In less than a second he was rending the Waldorf asunder and saying
25 what he thought of anybody who wanted to dine there.

But Mother was fully prepared to see him take it hard at the start. She paid no attention to his vehement refusals. She said brightly that the Waldorf was lovely and that it would do him good to go out. There was no dinner at home for him anyway, so what else was there to do?

When Father took in the situation, he undressed and put on his nightshirt. He shouted angrily at Mother that he had a sick headache. It made no difference to him whether there was any dinner or not. He couldn't touch a mouthful of food, he declared. Food be damned. What he needed was rest. After tottering around putting his clothes away, he darkened his room. He climbed into bed. He pulled up the sheets, and he let out his breath in deep groans.

These startling blasts, which came at regular intervals, alarmed Auntie Gussie. But when she hurried down to help, Mother seemed annoyed and shooed her back up.

The next thing she knew, Mother impatiently called up to her that she was waiting. She had got tired of scolding Father and trying to make him get out of bed, and had made up her mind to dine at the Waldorf without him. She and Auntie Gussie and Flossie marched off by themselves. But they had to come back almost immediately because Mother didn't have enough money, and when she rushed into Father's sick-room and lit the gas again and made him get up and give her ten dollars, his roars of pain were terrific.

Line 11. *adept:* expert
Line 11. *inveigling:* leading on by trickery
Line 24. *asunder:* apart

UNDERSTANDING THE SELECTION

Exercise 4.1: Close Reading

In the blank space, write the *letter* of the choice that best completes the statement or answers the question.

1. Mother wants to dine at the Waldorf because _____.

   (A) she is curious to see what the new hotel is like
   (B) Aunt Gussie and Cousin Flossie have asked to be taken there
   (C) she has not prepared dinner
   (D) she feels that Father deserves a change

2. When Mother presents her idea to Father, she expects that he will _____.

   (A) give in easily
   (B) never accept it
   (C) fight back hard at first
   (D) suggest going to a different restaurant

3. Father's deep groans ____.

(A) have no effect on anyone
(B) frighten Mother
(C) show he needed rest very badly
(D) are part of an act

4. The selection suggests that Father ____.

(A) does not lose his temper easily
(B) is fond of Aunt Gussie
(C) considers dining at the Waldorf a waste of money
(D) has a poor appetite

5. The narrator appears to be ____.

(A) ashamed of his parents
(B) siding with Father
(C) taking Mother's side
(D) trying to report the incident without taking sides

6. Father ____.

(A) doesn't care about food
(B) works uptown
(C) has an upstairs bedroom
(D) lives within walking distance of the Waldorf

7. Mother ____ of her objectives.

(A) achieves none
(B) achieves some
(C) is unwilling to give up any
(D) achieves all

8. Which of the following statements is UNTRUE? ____

(A) Mother leaves for the Waldorf with insufficient funds.
(B) Father turns off the electricity and darkens his room.
(C) The narrator explains what is happening in the minds of the characters.
(D) Flossie's character is not developed in the passage.

LEARNING NEW WORDS

Line	Word	Meaning	Typical Use
12	**coax** (v.) 'kōks	influence by gentle urging or flattery; persuade by soothing words; wheedle	The mother tried to *coax* her child to come in from play, but he paid no attention to her gentle urging.

		(*ant.* **bully**)	Use gentle words, not threats, as people do not like you to *bully* them.
10	**diplomatically** (*adv.*) ˌdip-lə-ˈmat-i-kə-lē	tactfully; without offending others	Some students hurt your feelings when they judge your work, as they do not know how to criticize *diplomatically*.
14	**impatient** (*adj.*) im-ˈpā-shənt	unwilling to bear delay or opposition; restless; short of temper	I asked them to wait a bit, but they were *impatient* and left quickly.
		(*ant.* **patient**)	Young children cannot bear delay, but as they grow older they become more *patient*.
39	**interval** (*n.*) ˈint-ər-vəl	space of time between two events; pause	There is an *interval* of four minutes between periods to permit students to go from one classroom to the next.
16	**mood** (*n.*) ˈmüd	state of mind; humor; disposition; temper	Dan said very little in class that day. He had just had a quarrel at home, and he was in a bad *mood*.
23	**placid** (*adj.*) ˈplas-əd	calm; peaceful; free of disturbance	While Joe obviously was disturbed by the news, his brother seemed *placid*.
		(*ant.* **agitated**)	Something must have been disturbing Eileen; she looked *agitated*.
24	**rend** (*v.*) ˈrend	pull apart violently; rip; tear	Pat is very displeased with the photograph. If she gets her hands on it, she will *rend* it to pieces.
41	**shoo** (*v.*) ˈshü	cause to move away; scare away; drive away	She *shooed* the flies away with a sweep of her hand.
17	**suspiciously** (*adv.*) sə-ˈspish-əs-lē	in a *suspicious* (distrustful) manner; distrustfully; in a way that shows a lack of confidence	One shopper watched the salesclerk *suspiciously* as he was checking out her groceries; she was afraid he might overcharge her.
27	**vehement** (*adj.*) ˈvē-ə-mənt	forceful; violent; showing strong feeling	The plan to do away with clubs and teams was dropped after *vehement* protests by students and parents.

Exercise 4.2: Sentence Completion

Which of the two choices correctly completes the sentence? Write the *letter* of your answer in the space provided.

1. If you are impatient, you are unlikely to _____ your temper.

    A. lose   B. control

2. A _____ is a popular interval with employees.

    A. coffee break   B. retirement plan

3. He looked back suspiciously, as if he _____ us.

    A. had confidence in   B. didn't trust

4. The lake was so placid that _____.

    A. there was not a ripple on it   B. our boat was tossed about quite a bit

5. If you shoo away the pigeons, they will _____.

    A. eat out of your hand   B. only come back

6. When Derek returned the following fall, we noticed a change in his mood; he _____.

    A. had grown quite a bit   B. seemed much friendlier

7. You handled the matter diplomatically; no one was _____.

    A. offended   B. pleased

8. If coaxing fails, I may have to use _____.

    A. threats   B. flattery

9. This tale will rend _____.

    A. your heart   B. a great deal of interest

10. Her vehement reply _____.

    A. showed she was angry   B. could hardly be heard

Exercise 4.3: Definitions

Each expression below defines a word taught on pages 44–45. Enter that word in the space provided.

_____ **1.** space of time between two events

_____ **2.** showing strong feeling

_____ 3. without offending others

_____ 4. pull apart violently

_____ 5. scare away

_____ 6. influence by gentle urging

_____ 7. in a distrustful manner

_____ 8. free of disturbance

_____ 9. unwilling to bear delay

_____ 10. state of mind

Exercise 4.4:   Synonyms and Antonyms

Fill the blanks in column A with the required synonyms or antonyms, selecting them from column B.

	Column A	Column B
_____	1. synonym for *disposition*	rend
_____	2. antonym for *patient*	diplomatically
_____	3. synonym for *rip*	vehement
_____	4. synonym for *tactfully*	interval
_____	5. synonym for *scare away*	placid
_____	6. antonym for *bully*	shoo
_____	7. synonym for *pause*	mood
_____	8. synonym for *distrustfully*	coax
_____	9. antonym for *agitated*	suspiciously
_____	10. synonym for *forceful*	impatient

LEARNING SOME ROOTS AND DERIVATIVES

Each word in bold type is a *root*. The words below it are its *derivatives*.

diplomat *(n.)*	You need the skill of a *diplomat* to keep opposing groups from fighting one another.
diplomatic *(adj.)*	You have to be *diplomatic* to maintain peace between opposing groups.
diplomatically *(adv.)*	You must be able to deal *diplomatically* with opposing groups.
diplomacy *(n.)*	It takes *diplomacy* to get opposing sides to work together.

impatient *(adj.)*	The audience was *impatient* for the film to begin.
impatiently *(adv.)*	The audience waited *impatiently* for the film to begin.
impatience *(n.)*	A few in the audience expressed their *impatience* by whistling.
mood *(n.)*	Why are you in a bad *mood*?
moody *(adj.)*	Why are you so *moody*?
placid *(adj.)*	She remained *placid* throughout the emergency.
placidly *(adv.)*	She continued to work *placidly* despite the trouble outside.
placidity *(n.)*	She was able to maintain her *placidity* all through the crisis.
rend *(v.)*	Baby's tears can *rend* a parent's heart.
rent *(n.)*	Baby's tearful plea can make a *rent* in Mother's heart.
suspect *(v.)*	Why do you *suspect* me?
suspicious *(adj.)*	Why are you *suspicious* of me?
suspiciously *(adv.)*	Why do you regard me *suspiciously*?
suspicion *(n.)*	Why do you look on me with *suspicion*?
suspect *(n.)*	Why do you consider me a *suspect*?
vehement *(adj.)*	I made a *vehement* denial of the charges against me.
vehemently *(adv.)*	I *vehemently* denied that I was in any way to blame.
vehemence *(n.)*	I asserted my innocence with *vehemence*.

Exercise 4.5: Roots and Derivatives

Fill each blank with the root or derivative just listed that best completes the sentence.

1. Philip is entirely trustworthy. We have no reason to _____ him.

2. I could tell that Jane was in a hurry because she kept looking at her watch _____.

3. An ambassador is a(n) _____ of the highest rank.

4. How can you sit here reading so _____ when there is so much screaming and shouting in the room?

5. The _____ in the beach umbrella will get larger if it isn't patched soon.

6. When Mitchell's sister tried to switch the TV to another channel, he objected so _____ that she gave up the attempt.

7. In trying to settle a quarrel, you should not say anything that might offend either side. Be _____.

8. The captain was _____; he was subject to fits of temper.

9. War must be replaced by peace, _____ by trust, and hate by love.

10. My friend showed his _____ by shouting, "Hurry up! I can't wait for you all day!"

Exercise 4.6: Defining Roots and Derivatives

Enter the word from pages 47–48 that best matches the definition below.

1. forcefulness _____

2. distrustful _____

3. often in bad humor _____

4. peaceful _____

5. a lack of trust _____

6. person imagined to be guilty _____

7. tact _____

8. opening resulting from tearing _____

9. in a forceful manner _____

10. tactful _____

IMPROVING YOUR SPELLING: SUFFIXES AFTER -CE AND -GE

1. If a word ends in -CE or -GE, and the suffix added to it begins with A or O, do *not* drop the E.

notice + able = noticeable
manage + able = manageable
courage + ous = courageous

2. If the suffix begins with a vowel other than A or O, drop the E.

notice + ing = noticing
manage + er = manager

3. Of course, if the suffix begins with a consonant, do *not* drop the E.

manage + ment = management
service + man = serviceman

Exercise 4.7: Wordbuilding After -*CE* and -*GE*

Fill in the blanks.

1. change + able = _____
2. advantage + ous = _____
3. discharge + ing = _____
4. service + able = _____
5. manage + ing = _____
6. encourage + ment = _____
7. village + er = _____
8. replace + ing = _____
9. change + less = _____
10. replace + able = _____
11. outrage + ous = _____
12. peace + able = _____
13. enforce + ment = _____
14. change + ing = _____
15. exchange + able = _____
16. disadvantage + ous = _____
17. notice + ing = _____
18. recharge + able = _____
19. enlarge + ment = _____
20. enforce + able = _____

PRONOUNS AND THEIR USES

1. Many pronouns have more than one form, or *case*. The pronoun *I*, for example, also has the forms *me, my,* and *mine.*

I is used as a subject.

I saw Brenda.	(*I* is subject of the verb *saw.*)
Joe and *I* saw Brenda.	(*I*, together with *Joe*, is subject of the verb *saw.*)
Brenda is shorter than *I*.	(*I* is subject of the understood verb *am:* Brenda is shorter than *I am.*)

Me is used as an object.

    Brenda saw *me*.   (*me* is object of the verb *saw*.)

    Brenda saw Joe and *me*.   (*me*, together with *Joe*, is object of the verb *saw*.)

My and *mine* are used to show possession.

    This is *my* glove.

    This glove is *mine*.

The following outline sums up the different forms, or **cases,** of the personal pronouns:

I	II	III
As a Subject	*As an Object*	*As a Possessive*
(known as NOMINATIVE CASE)	(known as OBJECTIVE CASE)	(known as POSSESSIVE CASE)
I	me	my, mine
you	you	your, yours
he	him	his
she	her	her, hers
it	it	its
we	us	our, ours
they	them	their, theirs

2. A *preposition* is a word that relates the noun or pronoun following it to some other word in the sentence:

    He looked suspiciously *at* Mother. (The word *at* is a **preposition.** It relates the noun *Mother* to the verb *looked*.)

    She wants to dine *with* us. (The word *with*, too, is a **preposition.** It relates the pronoun *us* to the verb *dine*.)

3. The following are some frequently used prepositions:

against	except	of
among	for	on
at	from	to
between	in	with
by	into	without

4. A pronoun after a preposition must be in the objective case. (See Column II above.)

QUESTION: Everyone left except _____. (*I* or *me*?)

ANSWER: Everyone left except *me*.

EXPLANATION: The objective case *(me)* is required after the preposition *except.*

(Note that *except* is a preposition, just the same as *by* or *with.* A preposition requires the objective case after it. It would be just as wrong to say "except I" as to say "by I" or "with I.")

Everyone left except me.

QUESTION: The class agreed with Mary and _____. (*he* or *him?*)

ANSWER: The class agreed with Mary and *him.*

EXPLANATION: The pronoun *him,* together with the noun *Mary,* is the object of the preposition *with; with* requires the objective case *him* (not *he*).

HINT: In a sentence like the previous one, construct two sentences. Then combine them for the correct answer.

SENTENCE 1: The class agreed with Mary.

SENTENCE 2: The class agreed with *him* (not *he*).

ANSWER: The class agreed with Mary and *him.*

Exercise 4.8: Using Pronouns

I. Complete the sentence.

1. My folks bought tickets for Miriam and _____. (*I* or *me?*)
2. Are you taller than _____? (*he* or *him?*)
3. Nobody complained except _____. (*he* or *him?*)
4. The committee consists of Kathy, Angela, and _____. (*I* or *me?*)
5. All expenses will be shared equally by you and _____. (*we* or *us?*)
6. Rhonda knows you can play the piano better than _____. (*she* or *her?*)
7. You and _____ have always gotten along well. (*they* or *them?*)
8. Wanda invited Terry and _____ to her party. (*I* or *me?*)
9. The Martins live on the same street as _____. (*we* or *us?*)
10. Has there been a quarrel between you and _____? (*they* or *them?*)

II. Fill in the missing forms of the italicized pronoun.

1. These are *my* notes. Give them to _____. They are _____, not yours.
2. This is *our* equipment. _____ own it. It belongs to _____. It is _____.
3. Let *them* sit in _____ own seats. These seats are ours, not _____.

4. *You* know what _____ share is. Marie and I have taken ours; the rest is

_____ .

5. *She* asked to use my calculator because _____ is out of order, but I told

_____ that I need it myself.

IMPROVING YOUR COMPOSITION SKILLS: DESCRIBING ACTION IN STORYTELLING

In telling a story, Clarence Day describes not only action that can be seen, but also action that cannot be seen. Reread the following paragraph.

> **One day while Father was in his office downtown, Auntie Gussie and Cousin Flossie arrived. Mother immediately began planning to take them to dine at the Waldorf, a much-talked-of new hotel at Fifth Avenue and Thirty-third Street, which she very much wanted to see. She knew Father mightn't like the idea, but he would enjoy himself after he got there, and she thought she could manage him.**

Question: How is the above paragraph organized?

Answer: Sentence 1 describes visible action—the arrival of Auntie Gussie and Cousin Flossie.

Sentences 2 and 3 describe invisible action—the thoughts in Mother's mind triggered by the arrival of the guests.

Exercise 4.9: Describing Visible and Invisible Action

Write a short paragraph describing a visible event that sets off an invisible reaction in somebody's mind. Use the above passage as a model.

Hints for Visible Events:

It is foggy, or snowing, or raining, when you get up in the morning.

A notice at the box office tells you that a performance or game you want to attend has been sold out.

An ambulance, fire engine, or moving van passes you on your way home and turns into your street.

Sample Paragraph

As I was coming home, an ambulance with siren screaming raced past me and turned into the street where we live. Instantly, I was alarmed. Could it be that someone in a neighbor's house—or even in my family—was seriously ill and needed help? I couldn't wait to get home.

Now write your paragraph.

_____

_____

_____

_____

_____

_____

_____

_____

_____

_____

Review I.1: Vocabulary and Spelling

Fill in the missing letters of the word at the right of the definition. (Each space stands for one missing letter.) Then write the complete word in the blank space.

	DEFINITION	WORD	COMPLETE WORD
1.	space of time	INTER __ __ __	_____
2.	person very greatly admired	__ D __ L	_____
3.	article of clothing	G __ __ MENT	_____
4.	scare away	__ __ OO	_____
5.	in a misleading way	DE __ __ __ TIVELY	_____
6.	object thrown at a target	__ __ SSILE	_____
7.	sleep lightly	D __ Z __	_____
8.	nervous laugh	T __ TT __ R	_____
9.	covered with thick rough hair	SH __ __ GY	_____
10.	fill with bewildered wonder	AST __ __ ND	_____
11.	very nearly	PR __ __ TICALLY	_____
12.	showing strong feeling	VEH __ __ __ NT	_____
13.	something required	__ __ __ ESSITY	_____
14.	shelter from danger	__ __ FUGE	_____
15.	to a large extent	CONS __ __ __ RABLY	_____
16.	hang down	__ __ OOP	_____
17.	in a distrustful manner	__ __ __ PICIOUSLY	_____
18.	unwilling to bear delay	IMP __ __ __ ENT	_____
19.	tactful person	__ __ __ LOMAT	_____
20.	right or left side of a formation	FL __ __ K	_____

Review I.2: Synonyms

To each line below, add a word that has the *same meaning* as the first two words on the line. Choose your words from the vocabulary list below.

1. calm; peaceful _____

2. unoccupied; empty _____

3. obstacle; hindrance _____

4. face; oppose _____

5. rip; tear _____

6. sadden; discourage _____

7. resentment; hostility _____

8. expected; probable _____

9. humor; disposition _____

10. puzzle; perplex _____

Vocabulary List

rend	baffle
animosity	depress
vacant	confront
placid	prospective
mood	obstruction

Review I.3: Antonyms

For each italicized word in column A, write the best *antonym* from column B.

		Column A	Column B
_____	1.	feeling of *shame*	imaginative
_____	2.	labored *effectively*	coax
_____	3.	if costs *increase*	foolhardy
_____	4.	entirely *believable*	indifferent
_____	5.	moved *sluggishly*	futilely
_____	6.	tried to *bully* us	diminish
_____	7.	*matter-of-fact* account	pride
_____	8.	a *wary* opponent	dense
_____	9.	seemed *eager*	briskly
_____	10.	*sparse* population	incredible

Review I.4: Proofreading

Each line contains one misspelled word. Spell that word correctly in the space provided.

_____ 1. aquainted, quantity, autumn

_____ 2. everyone, encouragement, exausted

_____ 3. surprise, bookeeper, noticing

_____ 4. morgage, teammate, library

_____ 5. probably, enforcable, nowhere

_____ 6. roomate, fascinate, salmon

_____ 7. nevertheless, playwright, reconize

_____ 8. hereafter, symtom, doubtful

_____ 9. receipt, goverment, someone

_____ 10. candidate, serviceable, outragous

Review I.5: Sentence Completion

Complete each sentence below with the most appropriate word from the following vocabulary list.

Vocabulary List

diplomatically	placid	obstruction
missile	practically	futile
baffled	foolhardiness	prospective
incredible	dozed	drooped

1. Jeff told the _____ story of having seen a lion on Main Street.

2. There was no movement of air. Flags _____. Not a leaf stirred.

3. Tickets for tonight's game are hard to get, as _____ all of them have been sold.

4. A double-parked delivery truck created a serious _____ to traffic.

5. From my father's _____ expression I could tell that he had not heard of my breaking the window.

6. The movie must have bored you, since you _____ through half of it.

7. When the boys brought their dispute to Mr. Greenburg, he settled it so _____ that neither side was offended.

8. The _____ landed several yards beyond the target area.

9. To have driven across the tracks as the speeding train was approaching would have been the utmost of _____.

10. The student's complaint was _____, as his teacher refused to change his mark.

Review I.6: Roots and Derivatives

On lines B and C, write the required forms of the italicized word on line A.

1. A. I am not a *deceiver*.
   B. I am not trying to _____ you.
   C. I am not trying to practice _____ on you.

2. A. Do not create an *obstruction* in our path.
   B. Don't be _____.
   C. Don't _____ our progress.

3. A. Belgium has a *dense* population.
   B. Belgium is _____ populated.
   C. Belgium has a high population _____.

4. A. Be *diplomatic*.
   B. Handle the matter _____.
   C. Use _____.

5. A. Wait. Don't be *impatient*.
   B. Don't be in a rush. Try to control your _____.
   C. There is no need to hurry. Stop behaving so _____.

6. A. Some people regard any change with *suspicion*.
   B. Some people are _____ of any change.
   C. Some people look _____ upon any change.

7. A. Is any tenant about to *vacate* an apartment?
   B. Will an apartment soon become _____?
   C. Will there be a _____ soon?

8. A. These problems are still *baffling*.
   B. These problems continue to _____ us.
   C. These are the same problems that have _____ us in the past.

9. A. Audrey is so *placid*. Nothing seems to disturb her.
   B. Audrey looked on _____ as my brother and I quarreled noisily.
   C. Nothing seems to disturb Audrey's _____.

10. A. Your grandfather moved very *briskly.*

    B. Your grandfather surprised us by his _____ of motion.

    C. Your grandfather took very _____ strides.

11. A. He did not realize the *futility* of trying to put out the fire by himself.

    B. He did not realize that it was _____ to try to put out the fire by himself.

    C. He _____ attempted to put out the fire by himself.

12. A. The news may *depress* them.

    B. They may find the news _____ .

    C. The news may give them a feeling of _____ .

13. A. Higher costs will make a tax increase *necessary.*

    B. Higher costs will _____ a tax increase.

    C. Increased taxes will become a _____ if costs continue to rise.

14. A. His *vehement* "no" showed that he was angry.

    B. His anger showed itself by the _____ with which he turned down our request.

    C. He _____ refused our request.

15. A. Light travels at the *incredible* speed of 186,000 miles per second.

    B. Light is _____ swift.

    C. Have you ever wondered at the _____ of the speed of light?

16. A. How can anyone remain *indifferent* to the sufferings of others?

    B. How can anyone regard the sufferings of others with _____?

    C. How can anyone look _____ on the sufferings of others?

17. A. The meteorologist now considers tomorrow as a *prospectively* rainy day.

    B. The _____ of rain makes our plans for tomorrow uncertain.

    C. The _____ rain may force us to change our plans.

18. A. So far, the detectives have found no one whom they regard *suspiciously.*

    B. So far, the detectives do not _____ anyone.

    C. So far, the detectives have no _____ .

19. A. The facts were in front of me all the time, but I didn't see them. I must have been *dense.*

    B. I remained _____ ignorant of the facts, though they were right before my eyes.

    C. I am ashamed of my _____ in failing to perceive the obvious facts.

20. A. It takes *diplomacy* to bring opposing sides together.

   B. You must be _____, if you are to bring the opposing sides together.

   C. If you are to get the opposing sides to agree, you must be a _____.

Review I.7: Concise Writing

Rewrite the following 97-word paragraph, keeping all its ideas but reducing the number of words. Try to use no more than 40 words.

> We would like to meet face to face with our old rivals, but they still regard us in a way that shows a lack of confidence. We understand their frame of mind. They have a fierce sense of their own worth and dignity. They are short of temper. But when others have suffered, they have not been without concern, interest, or feeling. The feeling of ill will that they have had toward us has to a large extent diminished. We might become friends. A year ago, such a possibility would have seemed too extraordinary to be believed.

Now write your version on the lines below. The first sentence has been rewritten to help you get started.

We would like to confront our old rivals, but they still regard us suspiciously.

_____

_____

_____

_____

_____

_____

_____

_____

_____

The Heart Is a Lonely Hunter

by Carson McCullers

Have you ever known anyone who could communicate only in sign language? Here are two such people.

IN THE TOWN there were two mutes, and they were always together. Early every morning they would come out from the house where they lived and walk arm in arm down the street to work. The two friends were very different. The one who always steered the way
5 was an obese and dreamy Greek. In the summer he would come out wearing a yellow or green polo shirt stuffed sloppily into his trousers in front and hanging loose behind. When it was colder he wore over this a shapeless gray sweater. His face was round and oily, with half-closed eyelids and lips that curved in a gentle,
10 stupid smile. The other mute was tall. His eyes had a quick, intelligent expression. He was always immaculate and very soberly dressed.

Every morning the two friends walked silently together until they reached the main street of the town. Then when they came
15 to a certain fruit and candy store they paused for a moment on the sidewalk outside. The Greek, Spiros Antonapoulos, worked for his cousin, who owned this fruit store. His job was to make candies and sweets, uncrate the fruits, and keep the place clean. The thin mute, John Singer, nearly always put his hand on his friend's arm
20 and looked for a second into his face before leaving him. Then after this good-bye Singer crossed the street and walked on alone to the jewelry store where he worked as a silverware engraver.

In the late afternoon the friends would meet again. Singer came back to the fruit store and waited until Antonapoulos was

²⁵ ready to go home. The Greek would be lazily unpacking a case of peaches or melons, or perhaps looking at the funny paper in the kitchen behind the store where he cooked. Before their departure Antonapoulos always opened a paper sack he kept hidden during the day on one of the kitchen shelves. Inside were stored various
³⁰ bits of food he had collected—a piece of fruit, samples of candy, or the butt-end of a liverwurst. Usually before leaving Antonapoulos waddled gently to the glassed case in the front of the store where some meats and cheeses were kept. He glided open the back of the case and his fat hand groped lovingly for some particular dainty
³⁵ inside which he had wanted. Sometimes his cousin who owned the place did not see him. But if he noticed he stared at his cousin with a warning in his tight, pale face. Sadly Antonapoulos would shuffle the morsel from one corner of the case to the other. During these times Singer stood very straight with his hands in his
⁴⁰ pockets and looked in another direction. He did not like to watch this little scene between the two Greeks. For, excepting drinking and a certain solitary secret pleasure, Antonapoulos loved to eat more than anything else in the world.

In the dusk the two mutes walked slowly home together. At
⁴⁵ home Singer was always talking to Antonapoulos. His hands shaped the words in a swift series of designs. His face was eager and his gray-green eyes sparkled brightly. With his thin, strong hands he told Antonapoulos all that had happened during the day.

Antonapoulos sat back lazily and looked at Singer. It was
⁵⁰ seldom that he ever moved his hands to speak at all—and then it was to say that he wanted to eat or to sleep or to drink. These three things he always said with the same vague, fumbling signs.

Line 34. *dainty:* something delicious

UNDERSTANDING THE SELECTION

Exercise 5.1: Close Reading

In the blank space, write the *letter* of the choice that best completes the statement or answers the question.

1. Antonapoulos _____ .

   (A) has a weak character
   (B) is neat
   (C) pays no attention to his cousin's warnings
   (D) has many subjects to talk about

2. Singer _____ .

   (A) is fond of drinking   (C) is always in a hurry
   (B) has very little to say   (D) seems intelligent

3. The two friends not only leave for work together but also _____.

 (A) work for the same employer
 (B) have lunch together
 (C) come home together
 (D) tell each other all that happened during the day

4. The owner of the fruit store _____.

 (A) watches Antonapoulos to prevent him from taking anything
 (B) is very unfair to Antonapoulos
 (C) knows that Antonapoulos is stealing, but does not try to stop him
 (D) does not know that Antonapoulos is stealing

5. Antonapoulos _____.

 (A) is a hard worker
 (B) shows laziness both at home and at work
 (C) is lazy at home but not at work
 (D) is lazy at work but not at home

6. Singer surpasses Antonapoulos in all of the following EXCEPT _____.

 (A) showing friendly concern and devotion
 (B) height
 (C) shaping words
 (D) love of food

7. The author is NOT specific in her description of _____.

 (A) Antonapoulos's job responsibilities
 (B) Singer's clothes
 (C) Singer's eyes
 (D) Antonapoulos's clothes

8. The passage devotes more attention to _____.

 (A) Singer than to Antonapoulos
 (B) the friends' similarities than to their differences
 (C) Singer's job than to his home life
 (D) the friends' differences than to their similarities

LEARNING NEW WORDS

Line	Word	Meaning	Typical Use
27	**departure** (n.) di-'pär-chər	act of going away; leaving; setting out	Our *departure* from the airport was delayed for two hours because of fog.

		(*ant.* **arrival**)	My aunt and uncle greeted me warmly on my *arrival* at their home.
34	**grope** (*v.*) ′grōp	search blindly or uncertainly; feel one's way	We *groped* our way slowly down the darkened stairs.
11	**immaculate** (*adj.*) im-′ak-yə-lət	spotless; absolutely clean	There was not a speck of dirt or dust in the room; it was *immaculate*.
38	**morsel** (*n.*) ′mȯr-səl	small piece of food; bit; fragment	All that was left of the two-pound salami was a *morsel* of three or four ounces.
1	**mute** (*n.*) ′myüt	person who is *mute* (unable to speak); one who cannot or does not speak	*Mutes* are able to speak to one another through hand signs.
5	**obese** (*adj.*) ō-′bēs	extremely fat; stout; corpulent	One member of the comedy team was very slim, and the other was just the opposite—*obese*.
		(*ant.* **skinny**)	
46	**series** (*n.*) ′sir-ēz	group of similar things or events coming one after the other; sequence; succession	Each side has won three games. Today's contest will be the final and deciding game in the *series* of seven.
38	**shuffle** (*v.*) ′shəf-əl	1. move about from one place to another; shift	We stood on a long line, and as we moved up, we *shuffled* our baggage along with us.
		2. walk without lifting the feet	Near the end of the hike we were so weary that we *shuffled* rather than walked.
11	**soberly** (*adv.*) ′sō-bər-lē	in a *sober* (plain) manner; not flashily	The son wore a flashy sports jacket and slacks of the latest cut, but the father was *soberly* dressed in a gray business suit.
		(*ant.* **gaily**)	Store windows are *gaily* decorated for the Christmas shopping season.
42	**solitary** (*adj.*) ′säl-ə-ˌter-ē	without companions; away from people; lonely	One of the most awful punishments a prisoner can suffer is to be placed in *solitary* confinement.

Exercise 5.2:   Sentence Completion

Which of the two choices correctly completes the sentence? Write the *letter* of your answer in the space provided.

1. The new shirt was as immaculate as _____.

   A. freshly fallen snow   B. a glove

2. The obese patient was advised by his physician to _____.

   A. eat between meals   B. go on a diet

3. You would not expect to find _____ in a soberly furnished room.

   A. plain furniture   B. bright colors

4. He needs a _____, not just a morsel.

   A. pair of sneakers   B. loaf of bread

5. My aunt lived a solitary life; she _____ had visitors.

   A. often   B. seldom

6. When we grope, we _____.

   A. cannot see our way clearly   B. cannot go astray

7. The following is a good example of a series: _____.

   A. spring, summer, autumn, winter   B. Better late than never

8. _____; don't be vague.

   A. Wait till we get there   B. Give us clear instructions

9. Don't shuffle; _____.

   A. lift your feet   B. take your time

10. A mute is unlikely to _____.

   A. read a newspaper   B. use a microphone

Exercise 5.3:   Definitions

Each expression below defines a word taught on pages 63–64. Enter that word in the space provided.

_____   **1.** a person who cannot speak

_____   **2.** a small piece of food

_____ 3. in a plain manner

_____ 4. extremely stout

_____ 5. away from people

_____ 6. search blindly

_____ 7. move about from one place to another

_____ 8. absolutely clean

_____ 9. act of going away

_____ 10. group of similar things coming one after the other

Exercise 5.4: Synonyms and Antonyms

Fill the blanks in column A with the required synonyms or antonyms, selecting them from column B.

	Column A	*Column B*
_____	**1.** synonym for *fragment*	grope
_____	**2.** antonym for *skinny*	departure
_____	**3.** synonym for *lonely*	mute
_____	**4.** antonym for *arrival*	shuffle
_____	**5.** synonym for *succession*	obese
_____	**6.** antonym for *gaily*	immaculate
_____	**7.** synonym for *shift*	soberly
_____	**8.** synonym for *feel one's way*	morsel
_____	**9.** synonym for *absolutely clean*	series
_____	**10.** synonym for *one unable to speak*	solitary

LEARNING SOME ROOTS AND DERIVATIVES

Each word in bold type is a **root**. The words below it are its **derivatives**.

depart *(v.)*	Your bus *departs* for Boston at 9:10 tomorrow morning.
departure *(n.)*	I will be at the terminal to see you before your *departure*.
immaculate *(adj.)*	Mrs. Kelly is an *immaculate* housekeeper.
immaculately *(adv.)*	Her home is *immaculately* maintained.
immaculateness *(n.)*	She prides herself on her *immaculateness*.

mute *(adj.)*	Ann made no reply; she was *mute* to all my inquiries.
mutely *(adv.)*	When I questioned her, she stared *mutely* at the ceiling.
mute *(n.)*	"Surely," I said, "you have the power of speech. You are not a *mute.*"
muteness *(n.)*	At last she broke her *muteness* and said: "Go away."
obese *(adj.)*	Some may become *obese* from overeating.
obesity *(n.)*	Overeating may cause *obesity.*
series *(n.)*	What is the next number in the *series* 2 . . . 4 . . . 6 . . . ?
serial *(adj.)*	In your report, page 5 comes before page 4, and page 12 is before page 11. Please put your pages in *serial* order.
serial *(n.)*	Channel 3 will do a *serial* on the adventures of Sherlock Holmes on Fridays at 8:30 P.M.
serialize *(v.)*	Channel 3 will *serialize* the adventures of Sherlock Holmes on Fridays at 8:30 P.M.
sober *(adj.)*	A Caribbean cruise on a luxury liner would not appeal to my uncle; he is a person of *sober* tastes.
soberly *(adv.)*	He prefers to live *soberly.*
soberness *(n.)*	A visit to a nightclub or a gambling casino would be out of keeping with the *soberness* of his way of life.
solitary *(adj.)*	At night, the building will be deserted, save for a *solitary* caretaker.
solitude *(n.)*	He expects to have a dog with him to reduce his *solitude.*

Exercise 5.5: Roots and Derivatives

Fill each blank below with the root or derivative just listed that best completes the sentence.

1. When you feel that you have been unfairly treated, speak up. Don't remain

   _____ .

2. Most people do not enjoy _____; they prefer to be with others.

3. Mom thought the tie I wanted to get Dad was too loud. She urged me to select a more

   _____ pattern.

4. The curtains were returned by the cleaner _____ laundered.

5. Before you _____, we will call to say good-bye.

6. Helen Keller was stricken with blindness, deafness, and _____

   when she was less than two years old.

7. At the factory, each new appliance receives a(n) _____ number in the order of its manufacture.

8. Overeating may lead to _____.

9. The magazine will _____ the new novel by printing successive installments in the next six issues.

10. "If you visit our kitchens," said the restaurant owner, "you will be impressed with their _____."

IMPROVING YOUR SPELLING: FORMING PLURALS OF NOUNS ENDING IN -F OR -FE

1. Some nouns ending in F or FE form the plural in the regular way by adding S.

SINGULAR	PLURAL
belief	belief*s*
safe	safe*s*

Exercise 5.6: Regular Plurals

Here are some more nouns that form the plural regularly. Write the plural in the space at the right.

brief _____

chief _____

giraffe _____

grief _____

handkerchief _____

proof _____

roof _____

sheriff _____

staff _____

2. Some nouns ending in F or FE change the F or FE to V and add ES.

SINGULAR	PLURAL
lea*f*	lea*ves*
kni*fe*	kni*ves*

Exercise 5.7: Irregular Plurals

Here are some more nouns that form the plural in the same way as *leaf* and *knife*. Write the plural in the space at the right.

calf   _____

half   _____

life   _____

loaf   _____

self   _____

shelf   _____

thief   _____

wife   _____

wolf   _____

Exercise 5.8: Using Plurals

Complete each sentence by writing the plural of an appropriate noun listed on pages 68–69.

1. How many _____ of bread can you buy for five dollars?

2. In the early autumn the _____ begin to fall.

3. Our library now has more than 8,000 books on its _____ .

4. Surely you don't believe that a cat has nine _____ ?

5. Banks store cash in their vaults and _____ .

6. Some watched the parade from the _____ of their homes.

7. Do you know how to arrange spoons, forks, and _____ when setting a table?

8. Considerate people use their _____ to cover their coughs and sneezes.

9. Before coming to America, the Puritans suffered because of their religious

   _____ .

10. The _____ of the police and fire departments were called to a meeting at City Hall.

Learn the difference between *loose* and *lose*.

Loose means "free," or "not fastened."

"In the summer he would come out wearing a yellow or green polo shirt stuffed sloppily into his trousers in front and hanging *loose* behind."

To *lose* means "to mislay," "be deprived of," "fail to get," or "fail to win."

How did you *lose* your wallet?

Exercise 5.9: *Loose* or *Lose*?

1. Tighten the handle; it's _____ .
2. Stand in line, or you may _____ your turn.
3. Win or _____ , we shall still be friends.
4. Junior made us look at his _____ tooth.
5. Plant in the spring, when the soil is _____ .
6. The Greens are moving. We are sorry to _____ them.
7. Was the dog _____ , or on a leash?
8. With these directions, you cannot _____ your way.
9. Did you _____ your homework again?
10. What would happen if the lion were to break _____ ?

IMPROVING YOUR COMPOSITION SKILLS: COMPARING TWO PERSONS

On page 62, Carson McCullers compares the way Singer and Antonapoulos participate when conversing at home:

At home Singer was always talking to Antonapoulos. His hands shaped the words in a swift series of designs. His face was eager and his gray-green eyes sparkled brightly. With his thin, strong hands he told Antonapoulos all that had happened during the day.

Antonapoulos sat back lazily and looked at Singer. It was seldom that he ever moved his hands to speak at all—and then it was to say that he wanted to eat or to sleep or to drink. These three things he always said with the same vague, fumbling signs.

Comment: The first paragraph describes what Singer said and how he said it. The second does the same for Antonapoulos. The resulting comparison offers a clear picture of each friend's speaking ability and personality.

Exercise 5.10: Composition

Compare how two people behave when they are both in the same situation—for example, when they:

> take part in a conversation, or
> are guests at a party, or
> are asked to make a charitable contribution, or
> are waiting for a bus, or
> are standing on a long checkout line, or
> are about to pay for what they are buying.

Use a separate paragraph for each person. A model answer follows.

Two Shoppers

> **It was interesting to see how customers behaved at the checkout counter. One shopper cautiously watched the display screen as his groceries were being priced. Before paying, he carefully examined his sales slip. When handed his change, he counted it twice before putting it into his wallet.**
>
> **Another shopper did not even look to see what she was being charged. Instead, she helped the salesclerk bag her order. When she got her change, she put the bills and coins into her purse without counting them.**

Now write your two paragraphs.

_____

_____

_____

_____

_____

_____

_____

_____

_____

_____

_____

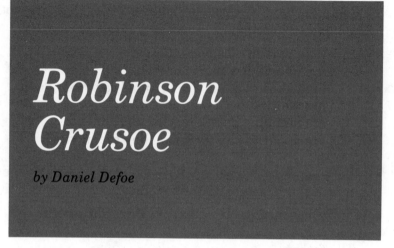

Robinson Crusoe

by Daniel Defoe

What would your folks say if they learned you were planning to leave home to see the world? In the following passage, Robinson Crusoe tells how his father reacted in a similar situation.

After this, he pressed me earnestly, and in the most affectionate manner, not to play the young man, not to precipitate myself into miseries which Nature and the station of life I was born in seemed to have provided against; that I was under no
5　necessity of seeking my bread; that he would do well for me, and endeavor to enter me fairly into the station of life which he had been just recommending to me; and that if I was not very easy and happy in the world, it must be my mere fate or fault that must hinder it, and that he should have nothing to answer for, having
10　thus discharged his duty in warning me against measures which he knew would be to my hurt. In a word, that as he would do very kind things for me if I would stay and settle at home as he directed, so he would not have so much hand in my misfortunes as to give me any encouragement to go away. And to close all, he told me I
15　had my elder brother for an example, to whom he had used the same earnest persuasions to keep him from going into the Low Country wars, but could not prevail, his young desires prompting him to run into the army where he was killed; and though he said he would not cease to pray for me, yet he would venture to say to
20　me that if I did take this foolish step, God would not bless me, and I would have leisure hereafter to reflect upon having neglected his counsel when there might be none to assist in my recovery.

I observed in this last part of his discourse, which was truly prophetic, though I suppose my father did not know it to be so
25 himself; I say, I observed the tears run down his face very plentifully, and especially when he spoke of my brother who was killed; and that when he spoke of my having leisure to repent, and none to assist me, he was so moved that he broke off the discourse and told me his heart was so full he could say no more to me.

Line 2. *precipitate:* hurl

UNDERSTANDING THE SELECTION

Exercise 6.1: Close Reading

In the blank space, write the *letter* of the choice that best completes the statement or answers the question.

1. The father _____.

   (A) does not try to influence Robinson's thinking
   (B) has stopped mourning for Robinson's elder brother
   (C) is not able to hide his feelings
   (D) makes no predictions about Robinson's future

2. The passage suggests that the Crusoe family is _____.

   (A) not poor
   (B) unable to pay its debts
   (C) not highly respected
   (D) large

3. The elder brother of Robinson Crusoe _____.

   (A) followed his father's advice
   (B) went to sea
   (C) was forced to earn his own bread
   (D) became a soldier

4. As used in the first sentence, the phrase "to play the young man" most probably means to act _____.

   (A) after careful consideration
   (B) recklessly
   (C) like a coward
   (D) selfishly

5. According to the selection, which of the following is most likely to happen later? _____

   (A) The elder brother will return home.
   (B) The father will encourage Robinson Crusoe to leave home.

(C) The father will stop praying for Robinson Crusoe.

(D) Robinson Crusoe will suffer a great deal.

6. Which of the following statements about the father is NOT supported by the selection? _____

(A) He expresses himself with considerable skill.

(B) He is convinced that his advice to his son is absolutely correct.

(C) He is worried about his son's future.

(D) He is determined not to help a son who disregards his advice.

7. The father may appropriately be described as _____.

(A) alarmed and loving

(B) selfish and uncaring

(C) sensible and unemotional

(D) cold and domineering

8. Which of the following would make the best title for the selection? _____

(A) A Dutiful Son

(B) Thirst for Adventure

(C) A Warning

(D) A Father's Blessing

LEARNING NEW WORDS

Line	Word	Meaning	Typical Use
1–2	**affectionate** (adj.) ə-'fek-shə-nət	feeling or showing a great liking for a person or persons; loving; devoted; tender	At the airport, the soldier received an *affectionate* welcome by relatives who hugged and kissed him.
		(ant. **cold, undemonstrative**)	Mr. Farrel is proud of his children, though he doesn't show it openly. He is an *undemonstrative* person.
22	**counsel** (n.) 'kaun-səl	1. advice	You would not have made this error if you had followed my *counsel*.
		2. lawyer engaged in the trial of a case; attorney	Before answering the question, the witness conferred with his *counsel*.
10	**discharge** (v.) dis-'chärj	perform; fulfill; carry out	If elected, I will *discharge* my responsibilities to the best of my ability.

23	**discourse** (n.) 'dis-ˌkôrs	talk; conversation; communication of ideas by talking	It is usually better to have a face-to-face *discourse* than to write or telephone.
1	**earnestly** (adv.) 'ər-nəst-lē	in an *earnest* (serious; not playful) manner; seriously; zealously (*ant.* **frivolously**)	Ever since he failed the test, Jeff has been doing his assignments *earnestly*. Before selecting a career, give it serious consideration. Do not choose *frivolously*.
6	**endeavor** (v.) in-'dev-ər	try; make an effort; strive	The defeated candidate is not discouraged and will *endeavor* to win the next election.
17	**prevail** (v.) pri-'vāl	1. urge successfully (usually with *on* or *upon*); persuade 2. gain the advantage; win; triumph	I finally *prevailed* upon John to lend me his science notes. Before the fight, I thought the stronger of the contenders would *prevail*.
17	**prompt** (v.) 'prämpt	cause (someone to do something); move to action; provoke	My high fever and loss of appetite *prompted* my mother to call our physician.
24	**prophetic** (adj.) prə-'fet-ik	having the characteristics of a *prophecy* (prediction of the future); foretelling future events; predictive	Jules Verne's novel TWENTY THOUSAND LEAGUES UNDER THE SEA was *prophetic;* it foreshadowed the invention of the submarine.
27	**repent** (v.) ri-'pent	feel sorry for an error or sin; regret	Most dropouts later *repent* their decision to quit school.

APPLYING WHAT YOU HAVE LEARNED

Exercise 6.2: Sentence Completion

Which of the two choices correctly completes the sentence? Write the *letter* of your answer in the space provided.

1. That was a long discourse. I did not know you could _____ so much.

A. run   B. talk

2. The affectionate parent greeted her child with _____.

A. an embrace   B. silence

3. Something prompted Carl to leave the examination suddenly, but I do not know the
   ____ .

   A. cause   B. penalty

4. Paul repented his harsh remarks to his sister. He ____ .

   A. would not take back one word of it   B. wanted to apologize

5. When you needed counsel, there was no one to ____ you.

   A. advise   B. recommend

6. The ____ is the one who prevails.

   A. loser   B. winner

7. In the past I ____ , but now I am working earnestly.

   A. was very serious   B. joked most of the time

8. You said you would endeavor to do your best, but you haven't shown even the slightest
   ____ .

   A. effort   B. appreciation

9. Our mayor deserves to be ____ for discharging the duties of the city's top office.

   A. criticized   B. praised

10. What the coach said last year was prophetic. We have just won the championship,
    ____ .

    A. as he had predicted   B. in spite of his doubts

Exercise 6.3: Definitions

Each expression below defines a word taught on pages 74–75. Enter that word in the space provided.

_____   1. in a serious manner

_____   2. carry out

_____   3. feel sorry for an error or sin

_____   4. urge successfully

_____   5. move to action

_____   6. communication of ideas by talking

_____   7. showing a great liking for a person

_____   8. make an effort

_____   9. lawyer engaged in the trial of a case

_____   10. foretelling future events

Exercise 6.4: Synonyms and Antonyms

Fill the blanks in column A with the required synonyms or antonyms, selecting them from column B.

	Column A	Column B
_____	1. synonym for *regret*	prevail
_____	2. synonym for *conversation*	discharge
_____	3. antonym for *cold*	prophetic
_____	4. synonym for *triumph*	affectionate
_____	5. synonym for *advice*	earnestly
_____	6. synonym for *predictive*	repent
_____	7. antonym for *frivolously*	prompt
_____	8. synonym for *try*	counsel
_____	9. synonym for *perform*	endeavor
_____	10. synonym for *cause*	discourse

LEARNING SOME ROOTS AND DERIVATIVES

Each word in bold type is a *root*. The words below it are its *derivatives*.

affection *(n.)*	If you show Fido that you like him, he will give you a great deal of *affection*.
affectionate *(adj.)*	Fido is an *affectionate* dog.
affectionately *(adv.)*	Fido licks my hand *affectionately*.
counsel *(n.)*	When I needed advice, Denise kindly offered me good *counsel*.
counsel *(v.)*	It was thoughtful of her to *counsel* me when I needed advice.
counselor *(n.)*	I was glad to have her as my *counselor*.
discharge *(v.)*	At their inauguration, legislators must take an oath to *discharge* their duties faithfully.
discharge *(n.)*	In the *discharge* of their duties, legislators must be faithful to their oath of office.
earnest *(adj.)*	Bob was *earnest* when he said he would lend you the money; he wasn't joking.
earnestly *(adv.)*	Bob *earnestly* wanted to lend you the money.

earnestness *(n.)*	The proof of Bob's *earnestness* is that he brought the money the next day.
endeavor *(v.)*	This fall I will *endeavor* to get on the track team.
endeavor *(n.)*	If my *endeavor* fails, I will make a second attempt when tryouts are held again.
prophet *(n.)*	Alexandra cannot foretell the future, since she is not a *prophet.*
prophetic *(adj.)*	Some people, however, can predict what will happen; they have *prophetic* vision.
prophetically *(adv.)*	Washington *prophetically* warned us to stay out of entangling foreign alliances. For a young nation, it proved to be good advice.
prophesy *(v.)*	The "experts" *prophesy* we will lose the championship.
prophecy *(n.)*	We hope their *prophecy* does not come true.
repent *(v.)*	How can we forgive him if he does not *repent* his attempts to hurt us?
repentant *(adj.)*	If he were really *repentant,* he would have said that he is sorry for the way he acted.
repentantly *(adv.)*	He would have come to us *repentantly* and asked us to forgive him.
repentance *(n.)*	But he has not taken back one word of what he said against us; he has shown no *repentance.*

Exercise 6.5: Roots and Derivatives

Fill each blank below with the root or derivative just listed that best completes the sentence.

1. I will not venture to foretell the future, since I am no _____.

2. We thought Valerie would be sorry for the trouble she had caused, but she was not the least bit _____.

3. Harvey came to me for advice, but I felt I was not the right person to _____ him.

4. The umpires showed good judgment in the _____ of their duties.

5. Her first _____ ended in failure, but she will make another attempt.

6. The sisters are cold to each other. There seems to be no _____ at all between them.

7. After his mother became ill, the son felt a deep _____ for the suffering he had needlessly caused her.

8. My _____ advised me to take Spanish as my first foreign language.

9. I didn't vote for Steve because he is too frivolous. In my opinion he lacks the

_____ necessary to be a good leader.

10. The meteorologist's _____ of heavy showers proved accurate.

IMPROVING YOUR SPELLING: MORE ABOUT THE SUFFIX *-LY*

Robinson Crusoe relates that what his father had told him proved to be "*truly prophetic.*"

1. Note that the adjective *true,* contrary to what we might expect, drops its silent E before the suffix -LY:

true + ly = truly

Two more adjectives that behave the same way are *due* and *whole.*

due + ly = duly

whole + ly = wholly

2. Other adjectives ending in silent E do *not* drop that letter before -LY.

vague + ly = vagu*e*ly

affectionate + ly = affectiona*te*ly

3. But adjectives ending in a *consonant plus* -LE (*able, ample, gentle,* etc.) drop the final E and add only a Y.

probable − *e* + *y* = probably

4. Adjectives ending in Y change the Y to I before -LY:

happy + ly = happ*i*ly

Exceptions: slyly, shyly, dryly

5. Adjectives ending in -IC add AL plus LY:

prophetic + al + ly = prophetic*ally*

Exercise 6.6: Building Adverbs From Adjectives

The first adverb has been entered as a sample.

ADJECTIVE	ADVERB
1. immaculate	**immaculately**
2. whole	
3. necessary	
4. incredible	

5. specific _____

6. earnest _____

7. true _____

8. fatal _____

9. uneasy _____

10. democratic _____

11. respectful _____

12. diplomatic _____

13. abrupt _____

14. humble _____

15. due _____

16. regretful _____

17. considerable _____

18. shy _____

19. exceptional _____

20. magic _____

Exercise 6.7: Reducing Adverbs to Adjectives

The first adjective has been entered as a sample.

ADVERB	ADJECTIVE
1. unhappily	**unhappy**
2. gratefully	
3. tragically	
4. soberly	
5. prophetically	
6. wholly	
7. easily	
8. agreeably	
9. truly	
10. usually	
11. brutally	
12. duly	
13. ably	
14. futilely	

15. gradually   _____

16. terrifically   _____

17. sensibly   _____

18. outrageously   _____

19. slyly   _____

20. gently   _____

USING *GOOD* AND *WELL*

Robinson Crusoe's father promised to "do *well*" for his son.

1. Note that *well,* above, is an adverb. It modifies the verb *do.*

    Here are some more examples of the use of *well* as an adverb.

    > Lucy dances *well.* (adverb—modifies verb *dances*)
    > I know him *well.* (adverb—modifies verb *know*)

2. But *well* can be an adjective, too, meaning "healthy," or "not ill."

    > We are glad you are *well.* (adjective—modifies pronoun *you*)
    > My uncle is not a *well* person. (adjective—modifies noun *person*)

3. *Good,* on the other hand, is an adjective.

    > This is a *good* dinner. (adjective—modifies noun *dinner*)
    > The food tastes *good.* (adjective—modifies noun *food*)

4. Note that both of the following are correct:

    > I feel *good.*
    > I feel *well.*

    However, the two expressions do not have the same meaning.

    > *I feel good* means "I feel happy" or "in high spirits."
    > *I feel well* means "I feel healthy" or "in good health."

Exercise 6.8: *Good* or *Well?*

1. I didn't do too _____ in the tryouts for the baseball team.

2. Paul has a fever; he is not _____ .

3. The old car still runs _____ .

4. I felt _____ when I learned that I had passed all my subjects.

5. The food looks very _____ to me.

6. Do your younger brothers behave _____ when you have visitors?

7. The news sounds _____ .

8. She's just an acquaintance; I do not know her _____ .

9. The milk may have turned sour; it doesn't smell _____ .

10. Ever since his hip injury, Grandpa has not been able to walk too _____ .

IMPROVING YOUR COMPOSITION SKILLS: MAKING AN IDEA CLEARER WITH AN EXAMPLE

Note the organization of the father's plea to his son in the passage from *Robinson Crusoe* (page 72):

1. In lines 1–14, the father presents the idea that it would be foolish for the son to leave home in search of adventure.

2. In lines 14–18, the father makes that idea clearer by offering an example:

> "And to close all, he told me I had my elder brother for an example, to whom he had used the same earnest persuasions to keep him from going into the Low Country wars, but could not prevail, his young desires prompting him to run into the army, where he was killed."

Exercise 6.9: Using an Example

Present an idea in a paragraph of about four or five sentences. In the first two sentences, state the idea. In the remaining sentences, make that idea clearer with an example.

Hints for Ideas:

Some of us never learn from our mistakes.
"More expensive" does not necessarily mean "better."
First impressions are often misleading.
Animals sometimes amaze us by their intelligence.
It pays to compare prices before buying.

Sample Paragraph

> It is a good idea before making an expensive purchase to visit two or three shops to compare their prices for the merchandise you intend to buy. You will be surprised to learn how prices may vary. For example, last year my cousin bought a portable radio in a neighborhood store at list price. Later, she met someone who had bought exactly the same radio in a downtown shop for 50% off the list price.

Comment: The first two sentences present an idea. The rest of the paragraph makes that idea clearer with the help of an example.

Now write your paragraph.

_____

_____

_____

_____

_____

_____

_____

_____

_____

_____

_____

Treasure Island

by Robert Louis Stevenson

The boy telling the story has been instructed by the captain to watch for "a seafaring man with one leg." Therefore, when a blind stranger appears one day, the boy at first suspects nothing.

So things passed until, the day after the funeral, and about three o'clock of a bitter, foggy, frosty afternoon, I was standing at the door for a moment, full of sad thoughts about my father, when I saw someone drawing slowly near along the road. He was plainly
5 blind, for he tapped before him with a stick and wore a great green shade over his eyes and nose; and he was hunched, as if with age or weakness, and wore a huge old tattered seacloak with a hood that made him appear positively deformed. I never saw in my life a more dreadful-looking figure. He stopped a little from the inn,
10 and raising his voice in an odd sing-song, addressed the air in front of him, "Will any kind friend inform a poor blind man, who has lost the precious sight of his eyes in the gracious defence of his native country, England—and God bless King George!—where or in what part of this country he may now be?"
15 "You are at the Admiral Benbow, Black Hill Cove, my good man," said I.
"I hear a voice," said he, "a young voice. Will you give me your hand, my kind young friend, and lead me in?"
I held out my hand, and the horrible, soft-spoken, eyeless crea-
20 ture gripped it in a moment like a vise. I was so much startled that I struggled to withdraw, but the blind man pulled me close up to him with a single action of his arm.
"Now, boy," he said, "take me in to the captain."

25 "Sir," said I, "upon my word I dare not."

"Oh," he sneered, "that's it! Take me in straight or I'll break your arm."

And he gave it, as he spoke, a wrench that made me cry out.

"Sir," said I, "it is for yourself I mean. The captain is not what he used to be. He sits with a drawn cutlass. Another gentle-
30 man—"

"Come, now, march," interrupted he; and I never heard a voice so cruel, and cold, and ugly as that blind man's. It cowed me more than the pain, and I began to obey him at once, walking straight in at the door and towards the parlour, where our sick old bucca-
35 neer was sitting, dazed with rum. The blind man clung close to me, holding me in one iron fist and leaning almost more of his weight on me than I could carry. "Lead me straight up to him, and when I'm in view, cry out, 'Here's a friend for you, Bill.' If you don't, I'll do this," and with that he gave me a twitch that I
40 thought would have made me faint. Between this and that, I was so utterly terrified of the blind beggar that I forgot my terror of the captain, and as I opened the parlour door, cried out the words he had ordered in a trembling voice.

The poor captain raised his eyes, and at one look the rum went
45 out of him and left him staring sober. The expression of his face was not so much of terror as of mortal sickness. He made a movement to rise, but I do not believe he had enough force left in his body.

Lines 34–35. *buccaneer:* pirate

UNDERSTANDING THE SELECTION

Exercise 7.1: Close Reading

In the blank space, write the *letter* of the choice that best completes the statement or answers the question.

1. The boy who tells the story _____.

   (A) makes no effort to get away from the blind man
   (B) has never had any fear of the captain
   (C) has just lost his father
   (D) does as he is told, without protest

2. The blind man _____.

   (A) knows where the captain is staying
   (B) is a friend of the captain
   (C) frightens the boy, but does not hurt him
   (D) does not know the way to the "Admiral Benbow"

3. When the blind man appears before him, the captain _____.

   (A) is too drunk to recognize him
   (B) doesn't even look up
   (C) makes no attempt to move
   (D) suffers a severe shock

4. What frightens the boy most of all is the blind man's _____.

   (A) threat to break his arm
   (B) voice
   (C) demand to see the captain
   (D) appearance

5. The boy may best be described as _____.

   (A) selfish and cunning
   (B) untrustworthy and cowardly
   (C) fearless and reckless
   (D) trusting and polite

6. The only one of the following questions to which the selection offers a specific answer is _____.

   (A) What is the relationship between the blind man and the captain?
   (B) What is the reason for the blind man's visit?
   (C) How has the captain earned his livelihood?
   (D) Is the blind man armed with a concealed weapon?

7. There is no information about the setting in lines _____.

   (A) 1–4
   (B) 9–14
   (C) 15–16
   (D) 19–20

8. Which of the following is the best title for the selection? _____

   (A) Youth and Age
   (B) A Strange Visit
   (C) Evils of Drunkenness
   (D) Attack and Counterattack

LEARNING NEW WORDS

Line	Word	Meaning	Typical Use
10	**address** (v.) ə-'dres	direct one's words to; deliver a speech to; speak to	The President usually *addresses* the nation on radio and television when about to make an important announcement.

35	**cling** *(v.)* 'kliŋ	hold on tightly; hold fast; adhere; stick	Johnny couldn't swim, but he managed to keep afloat by *clinging* to the overturned boat.
35	**daze** *(v.)* 'dāz	stun; confuse and bewilder; stupefy	The challenger fell back, *dazed* by the blow.
8	**deform** *(v.)* di-'fȯrm	spoil the shape or appearance of; disfigure	It is a pity when a pretty face is *deformed* by thoughts of envy, hatred, or bitterness.
13	**native** *(adj.)* 'nāt-iv	1. belonging to a person because of his birth	Since Grandfather was born in Rome, his *native* land is Italy.
		2. inborn; natural	Robert Burns had very little schooling, but a high *native* intelligence.
		3. grown or having its origin in a particular region	My great grandmother was born in Peking. Her *native* land was China.
		(*ant.* **alien, foreign**)	The newcomer spoke only Portuguese. English to him was an *alien* tongue.
8	**positively** *(adv.)* 'päz-ət-iv-lē	extremely; absolutely; in a *positive* (definite) way	We were very tired when we set out, and by the time we got to our destination we were *positively* exhausted.
7	**tattered** *(adj.)* 'tat-ərd	1. torn to shreds; ragged	Rod returned from playing football, his face bruised and his clothes *tattered*.
		2. wearing torn and ragged clothes	Refugees streamed into the emergency relief center, many of them barefoot and *tattered*.
41	**terrified** *(adj.)* 'ter-ə-ˌfīd	filled with *terror* (intense fear); frightened very much; alarmed	When a snake glided across Cliff's path, he became *terrified*.
41	**terror** *(n.)* 'ter-ər	intense fear; dread	Before I learned to swim, I had a *terror* of the water because I had once nearly drowned.
21	**withdraw** *(v.)* with-'drȯ	1. draw back; go away; leave	If you want to *withdraw* from our committee, we will gladly permit you to leave.
		2. take back; remove	Please *withdraw* my name. I do not wish to be a candidate.

(*ant.* **introduce**) At the last session, our Congresswoman *introduced* four bills to control pollution.

APPLYING WHAT YOU HAVE LEARNED

Exercise 7.2: Sentence Completion

Which of the two choices correctly completes the sentence? Write the *letter* of your answer in the space provided.

1. The fans were dazed by the ____.

   A. fairness of the decision B. stunning upset

2. We tried to withdraw but there was no way to get ____.

   A. in B. out

3. He looked as terrified as if he had just seen a ____.

   A. ghost B. rainbow

4. Isn't it about time that you got rid of your tattered ____?

   A. sweatshirt B. pen

5. Your native language is the language of the country where ____.

   A. you live B. you were born

6. There is ____ chance she may change her mind, as long as she is not positively opposed to joining us.

   A. little B. some

7. Jack wanted to ____, but he had nothing to cling to.

   A. hold on B. let go

8. I would have addressed the audience if I had not ____.

   A. forgotten my pen B. been too nervous to speak

9. Most people wake up in terror when ____.

   A. they have a nightmare B. the alarm clock rings

10. Will the injured leg remain deformed or will it regain its ____?

    A. shape B. strength

Exercise 7.3: Definitions

Each expression below defines a word taught on pages 86–88. Enter that word in the space provided.

_____ **1.** spoil the shape of

_____ **2.** take back

_____ **3.** hold on tightly

_____ **4.** torn to shreds

_____ **5.** direct one's words to

_____ **6.** in a definite way

_____ **7.** belonging to a person because of his birth

_____ **8.** frightened very much

_____ **9.** confuse and bewilder

_____ **10.** intense fear

Exercise 7.4: Synonyms and Antonyms

Fill the blanks in column A with the required synonyms or antonyms, selecting them from column B.

	Column A	Column B
_____	**1.** synonym for *tattered*	daze
_____	**2.** synonym for *stupefy*	native
_____	**3.** synonym for *dread*	positively
_____	**4.** antonym for *alien*	terror
_____	**5.** synonym for *disfigure*	address
_____	**6.** synonym for *frightened*	withdraw
_____	**7.** synonym for *speak to*	ragged
_____	**8.** antonym for *introduce*	cling
_____	**9.** synonym for *absolutely*	terrified
_____	**10.** synonym for *stick*	deform

LEARNING SOME ROOTS AND DERIVATIVES

Each word in bold type is a *root*. The words below it are its *derivatives*.

address *(v.)*   Ms. Jocelyn Baker will *address* the Astronomy Club.

address *(n.)*   The topic of her *address* will be "The Hidden Side of the Moon."

daze *(v.)*   I was *dazed* when I heard that Berlinger's is going out of business.

daze *(n.)*   The news of Berlinger's closing left me in a *daze*.

deform *(v.)*   Before Jonas Salk's vaccine, infantile paralysis used to cripple and *deform* thousands of people every year.

deformed *(adj.)*   This disease struck Franklin D. Roosevelt and left him *deformed*.

deformity *(n.)*   The discovery of a vaccine against infantile paralysis has freed millions of people from fear of suffering and *deformity*.

positive *(adj.)*   Yesterday, I said that I "might" come. I was sorry I could not be more *positive*.

positively *(adv.)*   Now, I know that I *positively* cannot attend.

positiveness *(n.)*   Now, I can say with *positiveness* that I shall be unable to attend the meeting.

tatter *(n.)*   When Eric returned from his soccer game, his face was muddy and his clothes were in *tatters*.

tattered *(adj.)*   My mother will probably use Eric's *tattered* clothes for rags.

terrify *(v.)*   Horror films may *terrify* a young child.

terrifying *(adj.)*   Ghosts, witches, and monsters like Dracula and Frankenstein are *terrifying* to many children.

terrified *(adj.)*   *Terrified* youngsters sometimes scream while watching a horror film.

terror *(n.)*   For centuries, the Barbary pirates spread *terror* in the Mediterranean Sea.

terrorize *(v.)*   They *terrorized* the merchant vessels of those nations that did not pay them tribute.

terrorism *(n.)*   In 1815, an American fleet defeated the Barbary pirates, ending their *terrorism* against American shipping.

terrorist *(n.)*   The airplane hijacker is a twentieth-century pirate. Since he uses the passengers and crew as hostages, he must be considered a *terrorist*.

withdraw *(v.)*	Instead of joining in the conversation, Joe *withdrew* into a corner.
withdrawn *(adj.)*	I was surprised, because he is not usually shy or *withdrawn.*
withdrawal *(n.)*	Noticing his *withdrawal,* I went over to talk with him.

Exercise 7.5: Roots and Derivatives

Fill each blank below with the root or derivative just listed that best completes the sentence.

1. At first, Janet did not realize what she was doing; she must have been in a(n) _____ .

2. A beggar in _____ s appeared at the king's court.

3. A child, _____ by the smoke, was hiding under a bed, where fortunately a firefighter found him.

4. At first the new student was shy and _____, but he soon began to make friends.

5. The President's _____ will be on radio and television tonight.

6. When the _____ was arrested, a store of explosives was found in his basement.

7. You have not given us a very _____ statement of what you saw. Can you please be more definite?

8. Most banks will permit you to make a deposit or _____ by mail.

9. One of our teammates has a limp but plays well in spite of this _____ .

10. My first ride on a Ferris wheel was a(n) _____ experience. I was frightened to death.

IMPROVING YOUR SPELLING: DISTINGUISHING BETWEEN HOMONYMS

Homonyms are words that are alike in pronunciation but different in spelling and meaning.

Review these sets of homonyms:

> *brake* (stopping device): Step on the *brake.*
> *break* (fracture): How did you *break* your arm?
>
> *its* (belonging to it): The dog licked *its* paw.
> *it's* (it is): Can't you see *it's* raining?

pain (suffering): John complained about the *pain* in his arm.
pane (sheet of glass): Who broke the *pane* in the storm window?

passed (went by): She *passed* me in the corridor a moment ago.
past (beyond): Go *past* the next corner.
past (time gone by): Can you remember the *past*?

sight (vision): The old man has lost the precious *sight* of his eyes.
site (space of ground): Has a *site* been chosen for the new building?

straight (free from curves): A ruler has a *straight* edge.
strait (narrow waterway): Where is the *Strait* of Gibraltar?

there (in that place): When will you be *there*?
their (belonging to them): They ate *their* lunch.
they're (they are): They said that *they're* coming.

to (in the direction of and reaching): Jerry walks *to* school.
too (also): Gail wants to stop. Do you want to stop, *too*?
too (excessively): Open a window. It's *too* hot in here.
two (one plus one): The price is *two* dollars.

wait (delay): We can *wait* no longer.
weight (heaviness): Labels on packaged foods state the
                    weight of the contents.

your (belonging to you): "Will you give me *your* hand?"
you're (you are): Tell us what *you're* planning.

Exercise 7.6: Homonyms

Insert the correct choice.

1. I went _____ home. *(straight, strait)*

2. Have you gained any _____? *(wait, weight)*

3. Miss Stark liked my composition, except for _____ ending. *(it's, its)*

4. Months have _____ since I last saw him. *(passed, past)*

5. How much will it cost to replace the broken _____? *(pain, pane)*

6. Money has been voted to purchase an athletic field _____. *(sight, site)*

7. Are they bringing _____ gloves? *(there, their, they're)*

8. Do you realize what _____ saying? *(your, you're)*

9. Be careful not to _____ the point. *(brake, break)*

10. I'd like something to eat. Are you hungry _____? *(too, two)*

MORE ABOUT ADVERBS

"He was *plainly* blind . . ."

1. Most adverbs, like *plainly* above, are formed by adding *-ly* to the adjective.

ADJECTIVE   ADVERB

plain + ly = plain*ly*
real   + ly = real*ly*

2. Some adverbs do not add *-ly*. They are spelled the same as adjectives.

Lead me *straight* up to him. (adverb—modifies verb *lead*)
      ADV.

This is a *straight* line. (adjective—modifies noun *line*)
      ADJ.

Exercise 7.7: Adverbs Spelled Like Adjectives

Here are some additional words like *straight* that have the same spelling as adjective and adverb. Fill in the blank spaces in the adverb column.

	ADJECTIVE	ADVERB
SAMPLE:	straight	**straight**
	better	_____
	early	_____
	fast	_____
	hard	_____
	late	_____
	low	_____
	near	_____

3. Some adjectives give us two adverbs: (1) the same as the adjective, and (2) the adjective plus *-ly:*

(1) The blind man clung *close* to me.
(2) The blind man clung *closely* to me.

Exercise 7.8: Two Adverbs From One Adjective

Fill in the blank spaces in the adverb column.

	ADJECTIVE	ADVERB		
SAMPLE:	close	**close**	or	**closely**
	bright	_____	or	_____
	cheap	_____	or	_____
	deep	_____	or	_____
	fair	_____	or	_____
	high	_____	or	_____
	loose	_____	or	_____
	loud	_____	or	_____
	right	_____	or	_____
	rough	_____	or	_____
	slow	_____	or	_____
	smooth	_____	or	_____
	tight	_____	or	_____
	wrong	_____	or	_____

Exercise 7.9: Adverb Review

Each first sentence below has a word in italics used as an adjective. If the *same* word—with *no change* in spelling—can be used as an adverb, write it in the blank space in the second sentence. If not, write the form ending in *-ly*.

SAMPLE: It was a *close* race.
Stay **close** to me.

SAMPLE: Don is a *careful* worker.
Don does his work **carefully.**

1. It was a *bright* day.

The sun shone _____.

2. This is the *right* way to do it.

Do it _____.

3. Bea is a *skillful* speaker.

Bea speaks _____.

4. We took a *straight* route.

We went _____ home.

5. Write a *better* composition.

Can't you write _____?

6. The play was a *terrific* success.

The play was _____ successful.

7. It was a *slow* train.

The train went _____.

8. The nurses were *immaculate*.

The nurses were _____

dressed.

9. The plane was at a *low* altitude.

The plane was flying _____.

10. The cover should be *tight*.

The cover should fit _____.

11. The *whole* building was destroyed.

The building was _____ destroyed.

12. She spoke in a *loud* voice.

She spoke too _____.

13. Milk is *cheap*.

Milk can be bought _____.

14. You pronounced my name the *wrong* way.

You pronounced my name _____.

15. Joel has made *considerable* improvement.

Joel is _____ improved.

16. The strap was *loose*.

The strap hung _____.

17. This is a *true* pleasure.

We are _____ pleased.

18. We went to the *early* show.

We went _____.

IMPROVING YOUR COMPOSITION SKILLS: NARRATING AN INCIDENT

Let us recall how Robert Louis Stevenson begins his account of the incident on page 84:

> **So things passed until, the day after the funeral, and about three o'clock of a bitter, foggy, frosty afternoon, I was standing at the door for a moment, full of sad thoughts about my father, when I saw someone drawing slowly near along the road.**

Question: Why is this an excellent introductory sentence?

Answer: It tells us not only:

1. WHEN the incident occurred: "the day after the funeral . . . about three o'clock of a bitter, foggy, frosty afternoon."

2. WHO is doing the talking: "I" (the narrator).

3. WHERE the narrator is at the time: "I was standing at the door."

But it also tells us WHAT is happening in two places:

(*a*) in the mind of the narrator ("full of sad thoughts about my father") and

(*b*) on the road ("I saw someone drawing slowly near.")

All of the above helps to create an atmosphere of suspense, making us eager to learn what is going to happen next.

Exercise 7.10: Introducing an Incident

Write only the first sentence of an incident of which you are the narrator, using Stevenson's introductory sentence as a model. Tell when and where the incident took place, what was in your mind at the time, and what actually happened.

Sample Introductory Sentence

> **About four o'clock on a rainy afternoon in late August, as I was looking out the window of my room, unhappy that my summer vacation was almost over, I saw an unfamiliar car parked across the street from our building.**

Another Sample

> **Just before noon on a cool Sunday, as my friend and I were walking toward the outdoor flea market, looking forward to some great bargains and tasty refreshments, there was a sudden screeching of brakes, a crash, and a smashing of glass.**

Now write your introductory sentence.

_____

_____

_____

_____

_____

_____

_____

_____

_____

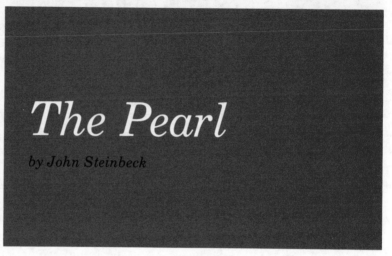

The Pearl

by John Steinbeck

Kino has a precious pearl to sell, but he cannot get a fair price for it in his own village. Therefore, with his wife Juana and their infant Coyotito, he has begun the long and difficult journey to Mexico City. Suddenly he discovers that he is being followed.

And then he saw them moving along. His body stiffened and he drew down his head and peeked out from under a fallen branch. In the distance he could see three figures, two on foot and one on horseback. But he knew what they were, and a chill of fear went
5 through him. Even in the distance he could see the two on foot moving slowly along, bent low to the ground. Here, one would pause and look at the earth, while the other joined him. They were the trackers, they could follow the trail of a bighorn sheep in the stone mountains. They were as sensitive as hounds. Here, he and
10 Juana might have stepped out of the wheel rut, and these people from the inland, these hunters, could follow, could read a broken straw or a little tumbled pile of dust. Behind them, on a horse, was a dark man, his nose covered with a blanket, and across his saddle a rifle gleamed in the sun.
15 Kino lay as rigid as the tree limb. He barely breathed, and his eyes went to the place where he had swept out the track. Even the sweeping might be a message to the trackers. He knew these inland hunters. In a country where there was little game they managed to live because of their ability to hunt, and they were
20 hunting him. They scuttled over the ground like animals and found a sign and crouched over it while the horseman waited.

The trackers whined a little, like excited dogs on a warming
trail. Kino slowly drew his big knife to his hand and made it ready.
He knew what he must do. If the trackers found the swept place,
25 he must leap for the horseman, kill him quickly and take the rifle.
That was his only chance in the world. And as the three drew
nearer on the road, Kino dug little pits with his sandaled toes so
that he could leap without warning, so that his feet would not slip.
He had only a little vision under the fallen limb.

30 Now Juana, back in her hidden place, heard the pad of the
horse's hoofs, and Coyotito gurgled. She took him up quickly and
put him under her shawl.

When the trackers came near, Kino could see only their legs
and only the legs of the horse from under the fallen branch. He
35 saw the dark horny feet of the men and their ragged white clothes,
and he heard the creak of leather of the saddle and the clink of
spurs. The trackers stopped at the swept place and studied it, and
the horseman stopped. The horse flung his head up against the bit
and the bit-roller clicked under his tongue and the horse snorted.
40 Then the dark trackers turned and studied the horse and watched
his ears.

Kino was not breathing, but his back arched a little and the
muscles of his arms and legs stood out with tension and a line of
sweat formed on his upper lip.

UNDERSTANDING THE SELECTION

Exercise 8.1: Close Reading

In the blank space, write the *letter* of the choice that best completes the statement or
answers the question.

1. When Kino sees the men in the distance, he realizes that _____.

    (A) they will not be able to find him
    (B) he has no chance to escape
    (C) they have been sent to find him and kill him
    (D) they know exactly where he is hiding

2. The author does NOT compare the trackers to _____.

    (A) sheep   (C) animals
    (B) hounds   (D) dogs

3. The trackers _____.

    (A) do not worry Kino
    (B) show signs of becoming discouraged
    (C) follow behind the horseman
    (D) look to the horse for a clue

4. The selection suggests that _____.

    (A) Juana is worried that Coyotito may betray their hiding place
    (B) the trackers have rifles
    (C) Kino is barefoot
    (D) there are many wild animals in the area

5. The expression "a warming trail," as used in the first sentence of the third paragraph, means a trail that _____.

    (A) is losing its freshness
    (B) leads into the sun
    (C) seems increasingly likely to be the right trail
    (D) becomes increasingly harder to follow

6. How many distinctly different sounds are described in lines 30–41? _____

    (A) five
    (B) four
    (C) six
    (D) three

7. All of the following are correct statements, EXCEPT _____.

    (A) The fear that grips Kino is not a paralyzing fear.
    (B) The trackers excel in following a trail.
    (C) The horse has an acute sense of hearing.
    (D) Juana and Coyotito are aware of their desperate situation.

8. Which of the following would be the best title for the selection? _____

    (A) Hunters and Their Prey
    (B) Footprints in the Sand
    (C) Fugitives from Justice
    (D) Lost in the Wilderness

LEARNING NEW WORDS

Line	Word	Meaning	Typical Use
15	**barely** *(adv.)* 'be(ə)r-lē	hardly; by the narrowest margin; scarcely	You turned the TV down so low that I could *barely* hear it.
21	**crouch** *(v.)* 'kraüch	stoop low with legs bent; bend low	Everyone stood straight except Tony, who was *crouching*, apparently to tie a shoelace.
18	**game** *(n.)* 'gām	animals hunted for sport or food; quarry	The hunters crouched in the tall grass, waiting for their *game* to appear.

15	**limb** *(n.)* 'lim	1. large branch of a tree	During the storm, a heavy elm *limb* fell on two parked cars, wrecking them.
		2. arm, leg, or wing	You say you fractured a *limb* last year? Was it an arm or a leg?
7	**pause** *(v.)* 'poz	stop temporarily; hesitate; wait	The pupil who read too quickly was advised to *pause* briefly at the end of each sentence.
15	**rigid** *(adj.)* 'rij-əd	stiff; not bending; inflexible; hard	Foam-cushioned seats are much more comfortable than *rigid* wooden benches.
		(ant. **flexible***)*	Plastic toys are not so *flexible* as toys made of rubber.
9	**sensitive** *(adj.)* 'sen-sə-tiv	1. receiving impressions readily	Our watchdog barks at the approach of strangers while they are still a good way off; she is a *sensitive* animal.
		2. easily affected or moved (usually followed by *to*)	Mom always stops to help when she sees someone in trouble. She is *sensitive* to the plight of others.
		3. easily hurt	Wayne is a very *sensitive* child; if you scold him ever so slightly, he will begin to cry.
		(ant. **insensitive, callous***)*	How can you be so *insensitive* as to quarrel with Kerwin when he is ill? Have you no feelings?
			I thought Tom might be hurt by my criticism, but I was wrong; he is quite *callous*.
43	**tension** *(n.)* 'ten-shən	1. stretched condition; degree of stiffness; tautness	Guitar strings break when tightened to an abnormal *tension*.
		2. state of mental unrest; nervous strain; stress	With the score tied and less than a minute to play, the *tension* on both sides was almost unbearable.
29	**vision** *(n.)* 'vizh-ən	power of seeing; sight	Since she began using her new glasses, Susan's *vision* has improved greatly.
		(ant. **blindness***)*	

22 **whine** (v.)   utter a high-pitched   My little nephew used to *whine*
   ʹhwīn   complaining cry or sound;   when he talked, so that he al-
                        complain in an irritable,   ways sounded as if he were com-
                        childish way   plaining.

APPLYING WHAT YOU HAVE LEARNED

Exercise 8.2: Sentence Completion

Which of the two choices correctly completes the sentence? Write the *letter* of your answer in the space provided.

1. I was under such tension that I _____.

   A. bit my fingernails   B. fell asleep

2. When game was plentiful, there was no shortage of _____.

   A. sports   B. meat

3. _____ may reduce a driver's vision.

   A. A dirty windshield   B. Worn tires

4. I crouched to _____.

   A. read the notice posted above the chalkboard   B. look at the titles on the bottom shelf

5. When a child whines, it may be a sign that _____.

   A. something is bothering him or her   B. he or she is happy and content

6. With an income of $161.75 and expenses of _____, our club last year barely managed to make ends meet.

   A. $187.50   B. $159.75

7. I did not injure a limb; I bruised my _____.

   A. leg   B. chin

8. If we pause, we shall _____.

   A. overtake the leader   B. fall behind

9. A _____ is not rigid.

   A. rubber band   B. brick chimney

10. Lou _____; he is very sensitive.

   A. does not care what others may say   B. is easily offended

Exercise 8.3: Definitions

Each expression below defines a word taught on pages 100–102. Enter that word in the space provided.

_____ 1. stop temporarily

_____ 2. state of mental unrest

_____ 3. not bending

_____ 4. receiving impressions readily

_____ 5. by the narrowest margin

_____ 6. animals hunted for sport or food

_____ 7. utter a high-pitched complaining cry

_____ 8. arm, leg, or wing

_____ 9. stoop low with legs bent

_____ 10. power of seeing

Exercise 8.4: Synonyms and Antonyms

Fill the blanks in column A with the required synonyms or antonyms, selecting them from column B.

Column A	Column B
_____ 1. synonym for *hesitate*	tension
_____ 2. antonym for *blindness*	limb
_____ 3. synonym for *stress*	rigid
_____ 4. synonym for *quarry*	whine
_____ 5. antonym for *flexible*	barely
_____ 6. synonym for *branch*	crouch
_____ 7. synonym for *hardly*	vision
_____ 8. antonym for *callous*	pause
_____ 9. synonym for *complain*	sensitive
_____ 10. synonym for *bend low*	game

Each word in bold type is a *root*. The words below it are its *derivatives*.

bare *(adj.)* — I made the deadline by *bare* seconds.

barely *(adv.)* — I *barely* managed to get my application in on time.

crouch *(v.)* — If I *crouch,* my back doesn't ache when I get up.

crouch *(n.)* — However, my father's back sometimes hurts him when he gets up from a *crouch.*

pause *(v.)* — Since we have been driving for nearly two hours, let us *pause* for some refreshment.

pause *(n.)* — After a brief *pause* for lunch, we will continue with our trip.

rigid *(adj.)* — Nancy is going to be *rigid* in sticking to her diet.

rigidly *(adv.)* — She has told me that she will *rigidly* avoid all fattening foods.

rigidity *(n.)* — She should certainly lose weight if she follows her diet with *rigidity.*

sensitive *(adj.)* — One of my teeth is painfully *sensitive.*

sensitively *(adv.)* — It reacts more *sensitively* to cold than to heat.

sensitivity *(n.)* — The dentist says that, after the tooth is treated, the *sensitivity* should disappear.

tense *(adj.)* — Some of the passengers became *tense* when their plane continued to circle over the airport, awaiting permission to land.

tensely *(adv.)* — The pilot, too, waited *tensely* for instructions from the control tower.

tension *(n.)* — If not for the fog, there would have been no delays and, therefore, no *tension.*

vision *(n.)* — People of *vision* try to make an educated guess of what conditions will be like in the future.

envision *(v.)* — They try to *envision* tomorrow's needs today.

revision *(n.)* — Their guess may need *revision*—it may be too high or too low—but it is better to plan ahead than to live blindly.

whine *(v.)* — Did you hear the wind *whine* through the trees?

whine *(n.)* — Listen to the *whine* of the wind.

Exercise 8.5: Roots and Derivatives

Fill each blank below with the root or derivative just listed that best completes the sentence.

1. I was very _____ when I began my speech; the nervous strain was almost too much for me.

2. In a race it is much better to start from a(n) _____ than from a standing position.

3. My teacher said that, looking ahead, she could _____ a bright future for me.

4. The batting championship was decided by the _____ margin of one thousandth of a percentage point.

5. Knowing your brother's _____, I was extremely careful not to say anything that might hurt his feelings.

6. Anyone could have seen that I was nervous as I paced _____ up and down the hospital corridor.

7. Your composition needs _____; you should look it over again to make corrections and improvements.

8. When troops are reviewed, they are supposed to stand _____ at attention.

9. The _____ of sirens was a sign that the fire engines were approaching.

10. After a brief _____ for a commercial, the program will continue.

IMPROVING YOUR SPELLING: WORDS ENDING IN -LE, -EL, -AL, AND -FUL

1. Words usually end in -LE, rather than -EL.

rifle	tumble	simple	ample
saddle	tickle	pickle	angle
muscle	bottle	candle	article
gurgle	sample	nozzle	particle
giggle	ankle	handle	wrangle
baffle	dwindle	shuffle	principle (rule)

Reading Selection 8: The Pearl

2. A few end in -EL.

label	barrel	gravel	travel
model	panel	quarrel	colonel
nickel	parcel	bushel	counsel (advice)
level	cancel	morsel	

3. Review these words ending in -AL.

sandal	final	brutal	gradual
metal	special	material	usual
fatal	original	general	mortal
approval	natural	actual	official
renewal	additional	arrival	principal (chief)

4. Adjectives end in -FUL, rather than -FULL.

awful	grateful
beautiful	useful, etc.

Exception: the adjective *full* itself.

Exercise 8.6: Proofreading

One word on each line is misspelled. Spell it correctly in the space at the right.

1. wonderful, special, nickle, bushel _____
2. gradual, quarrle, additional, full _____
3. barrel, angle, level, peacefull _____
4. dwindel, sample, useful, little _____
5. aweful, saddle, final, panel _____
6. brutal, tearful, sandle, model _____
7. usual, painfull, simple, muscle _____
8. careful, counsel, morsel, baffel _____
9. lable, hopeful, natural, handle _____
10. pickle, ankel, joyful, fatal _____

AGREEMENT OF SUBJECT AND VERB

1. A singular subject requires a singular verb. A plural subject requires a plural verb.

The *horseman was* not in a hurry.
The *trackers were* not in a hurry.
    (The singular subject *horseman* requires the singular verb *was*. The plural subject *trackers* requires the plural verb *were*.)

Kino knows his business.

The *trackers know* their business.

(The singular subject *Kino* requires the singular verb *knows*. The plural subject *trackers* requires the plural verb *know*.)

2. Note that verbs ending in *s* are usually singular: *is, was, knows, has, does, eats, sleeps,* etc.

3. Normally the subject comes before the verb. In the following cases, however, you will find the **subject after the verb:**

    a. In a question:

        Are the *boys* home yet? (The subject is *boys.*)
        V   S

    b. In a sentence beginning with *There is, There are, Here is, Here are,* etc.

        There *is food* on the table. (The subject is *food,* not *there.*)
            V   S

        Here *are* your *friends.* (The subject is *friends,* not *here.*)
            V   S

4. An *of*-phrase between a subject and its verb has no effect on agreement.

    A box of cookies is on the shelf.

Reading the above sentence without the phrase *of cookies,* we have:

    A *box is* on the shelf. (The singular subject *box* requires the singular verb
      S V
    is.)

Exercise 8.7: Making Subjects Agree With Verbs

In each sentence below there is a subject without a verb. If that subject is singular, select a singular verb for it. If it is plural, choose a plural verb. Write the correct verb in the space provided.

    1. Here *(is, are)* _____ a pint of blueberries.

    2. There *(was, were)* _____ three persons in Kino's family.

    3. *(Where's, Where are)* _____ your gloves?

    4. The supermarket *(doesn't, don't)* _____ open until 8 A.M.

    5. A bunch of carrots *(sells, sell)* _____ for twenty-five cents.

    6. *(There's, There are)* _____ several reasons for starting early.

    7. How much *(has, have)* _____ prices gone up?

    8. A flock of birds *(was, were)* _____ feeding in the meadow.

    9. *(Doesn't, Don't)* _____ she know the correct answer?

    10. One of our players *(seems, seem)* _____ to be hurt.

To make a description more effective, include words that appeal not only to sight but also to some other sense or senses. Note how John Steinbeck does this when he writes about Kino at the approach of the trackers and the horseman:

> **"He saw the dark horny feet of the men and their ragged white clothes, and he heard the creak of leather of the saddle and the clink of spurs."** (page 99, lines 34–37)

Question: What senses does Steinbeck appeal to in the above?

Answer: 1. Sight.   Steinbeck makes us see the trackers by words like "dark horny feet" and "ragged white clothes."

2. Hearing. He also makes us hear what is going on by words like the "creak" of saddle leather and the "clink" of spurs.

Exercise 8.8: Description With Sight and Hearing Words

Using Steinbeck's sentence as a model, write a one-sentence description that appeals to the senses of sight and hearing.

Hints for Topics:

An approaching fire engine, ambulance, or police vehicle
A power failure
A cat meowing, a dog barking, a bluejay screeching, etc.
Noisy garbage-collection trucks in the early morning
Waves pounding a beach
A storm

Sample Descriptive Sentence

> Awakened by a clap of thunder in the middle of the night, I heard the rain beating against the windowpanes and saw the trees swaying in the wind when the lightning flashed.

Now write your descriptive sentence.

_____

_____

_____

_____

_____

Review II.1: Vocabulary and Spelling

Fill in the missing letters of the word at the right of the definition. Then write the complete word in the blank space.

DEFINITION	WORD	COMPLETE WORD
1. spoil the shape of	DEF _ _ _	_____
2. feel sorry for an error or sin	_ _ PENT	_____
3. make an effort	END _ _ VOR	_____
4. animals hunted	_ _ ME	_____
5. torn to shreds	TAT _ _ _ ED	_____
6. absolutely clean	_ _ _ ACULATE	_____
7. move to action	PR _ _ PT	_____
8. frighten very much	_ _ _ RIFY	_____
9. state of mental unrest	TENS _ _ _	_____
10. urge successfully	_ _ EVAIL	_____
11. feel one's way	GR _ _ _	_____
12. power of seeing	_ _ SION	_____
13. intense fear	TER _ _ _	_____
14. large branch of a tree	_ _ MB	_____
15. complain in an irritable way	WHI _ _	_____
16. person who cannot speak	MU _ _	_____
17. foretelling future events	_ _ _ PHETIC	_____
18. stoop low with legs bent	_ _ OUCH	_____
19. direct one's words to	ADDR _ _ _	_____
20. walk without lifting the feet	_ _ UFFLE	_____

Review II.2: Synonyms

To each line on the next page, add a word that has the *same meaning* as the first two words on the line. Choose your words from the vocabulary list.

1. perform; fulfill _____

2. scarcely; hardly _____

3. sequence; succession _____

4. stun; stupefy _____

5. hesitate; wait _____

6. bit; fragment _____

7. stick; adhere _____

8. talk; conversation _____

9. extremely; absolutely _____

10. lawyer; attorney _____

Vocabulary List

series	barely
positively	discourse
discharge	morsel
cling	daze
counsel	pause

Review II.3: Antonyms

For each italicized word in column A, write the best *antonym* from column B.

	Column A	Column B
_____	1. *cold* greeting	sensitive
_____	2. at our *arrival*	soberly
_____	3. *callous* person	withdraw
_____	4. often *accompanied*	departure
_____	5. *alien* custom	rigid
_____	6. *introduce* a motion	affectionate
_____	7. becoming *skinny*	obese
_____	8. acted *frivolously*	native
_____	9. *flexible* plan	earnestly
_____	10. *gaily* decorated	solitary

Review II.4: Homonyms and Spelling

Fill in the missing letters of the incomplete word in column A. Then write the complete word in column B.

Column A	Column B
1. Ask them for th _ _ _ names and addresses.	_____
2. Mother has a pa _ _ ful headache.	_____
3. Please take some. I have t _ o much.	_____
4. Never ride in a car with faulty br _ _ _ s.	_____
5. I know Chicago. I used to live th _ _ _.	_____

6. Read the directions printed on the lab __ __.   _____

7. Poison! Fat __ __ if swallowed!   _____

8. Who is the princip __ __ of your school?   _____

9. Does the first question baff __ __ you?   _____

10. Who has two nick __ __ s for a dime?   _____

Review II.5: Plurals
Write the plural in the space provided.

11. leaf   _____

12. knife   _____

13. belief   _____

14. handkerchief   _____

15. thief   _____

Review II.6: Adverbs
Change each of the following adjectives to an adverb ending in -*ly*:

16. easy   _____

17. true   _____

18. terrific   _____

19. brutal   _____

20. whole   _____

Review II.7: Sentence Completion
Complete each sentence below with the most appropriate word from the following vocabulary list:

Vocabulary List

tattered	morsel	prompted
affectionate	immaculate	rigid
repented	groped	terror
crouched	addressed	sensitive

1. Our neighbors are very neat; their home is always _____.

2. As Van was about to make his first jump, the thought that his parachute might not open filled him with _____.

3. This morning's forecast of heavy showers _____ Linda to take her umbrella.

4. Peggy noticed that the room was getting colder before I did; she is more _____ to changes in temperature.

5. This stick is too _____ for a bow; find one that bends more easily.

6. When Joe lost his temper, he made some remarks that he later _____.

7. One day my mother hid my father's _____ wool muffler in the hope that he would buy himself a new one.

8. I _____ under the bed for my missing slipper, first with one hand and then with the other.

9. By the time Cora was ready for some cake, only a thin _____ was left.

10. A car whizzed by dangerously close to Chuck as he _____ to change a flat tire.

Review II.8: Roots and Derivatives

On lines B and C, write the required forms of the italicized word on line A.

1. A. The nephew got an *affectionate* reception.

 B. The nephew was received _____.

 C. The nephew was greeted with _____.

2. A. Mary read the selection without *pausing*.

 B. Mary did not _____ at all in her reading.

 C. Mary read the selection without a _____.

3. A. I was under *tension*.

 B. I waited _____.

 C. I was _____.

4. A. Did he *repent*?

 B. Was he _____?

 C. Did he show _____?

5. A. Weren't you *dazed* by the news?

 B. Didn't the news _____ you?

 C. Didn't the news leave you in a _____?

6. A. In a hospital, *immaculateness* is absolutely necessary.

 B. A hospital should be _____ maintained.

 C. A hospital must be _____.

7. A. Are the numbers in *serial* order?

   B. Are the numbers arranged in a _____?

   C. Are the numbers arranged _____?

8. A. Do you claim to be a *prophet*?

   B. Can you _____ who will win tomorrow?

   C. What is your _____ about the outcome of tomorrow's game?

9. A. She sat *mutely* as I asked question after question.

   B. She remained _____ to all my questions.

   C. She replied to my inquiries with absolute _____.

10. A. Paul prepares his work with *earnestness*.

    B. Paul does his work _____.

    C. Paul is an _____ student.

11. A. The Puritans had a reputation for *soberness*.

    B. They were _____ dressed.

    C. In their _____ way of life, there was no place for dancing and merrymaking.

12. A. The umpire *rigidly* clung to his decision.

    B. The umpire was _____ in sticking to his decision.

    C. The umpire adhered to his decision with _____.

13. A. Disease may make a person *deformed*.

    B. Disease may cause a _____.

    C. Disease may _____ a person's body.

14. A. Do you always speak in a *whining* voice?

    B. Do you always speak with a _____?

    C. Do you always _____?

15. A. We must not allow *terrorism*.

    B. We will not permit criminals to strike _____ into the hearts of peaceful citizens.

    C. We must not allow criminals to _____ peaceful citizens.

16. A. Alice has a *sensitive* ear for music.

    B. Alice listens to music _____.

    C. Alice has a _____ to good music.

17. A. Have you noticed that the child is *withdrawn*?

    B. Have you noticed that the child tends to _____ from others?

    C. Have you noticed the child's _____ from group activities?

18. A. Are you *positive* that you saw him there?

    B. Did you _____ see him there?

    C. Can you say with _____ that you saw him there?

19. A. You have failed in the *discharge* of your duties.

    B. You left without _____ your duties.

    C. You did not _____ your duties.

20. A. Wasn't the lightning *terrifying*?

    B. Weren't you _____ by the lightning?

    C. Didn't the lightning _____ you?

Review II.9: Concise Writing

Rewrite the following 113-word paragraph in the space provided, keeping all its ideas but reducing the number of words. Try to use no more than 70 words.

> The suspect, dressed in an absolutely spotless manner, arrived with his devoted and loving parents and the lawyer who had been engaged to defend him in the trial. When damaging evidence was presented, the parents said it was hard to believe, and they seemed very much frightened, but their son listened without saying a word. At no time did he appear to be sorry for what he had done. He was obviously not a person who is easily moved. The only time he showed any feeling was when the judge refused to dismiss the charges against him. It was then that he cried out in an irritable, childish way, "It ain't fair!"

_____

_____

_____

_____

_____

_____

_____

_____

Two Years Before the Mast

by Richard Henry Dana, Jr.

*Richard Henry Dana, Jr., was a seaman aboard the **Pilgrim** in 1835, when the following true incident occurred. The captain was about to whip Sam, a sailor with whom he had had an argument, when another seaman, John, the Swede, asked a question.*

"What are you going to flog that man for, sir?" said John, the Swede, to the captain.

Upon hearing this, the captain turned upon John; but, knowing him to be quick and resolute, he ordered the steward to bring the
5 irons, and, calling upon Russell to help him, went up to John.

"Let me alone," said John. "I'm willing to be put in irons. You need not use any force"; and, putting out his hands, the captain slipped the irons on, and set him aft to the quarter-deck. Sam, by this time, was *seized up,* as it is called; that is, placed against the
10 shrouds, with his wrists made fast to them, his jacket off, and his back exposed. The captain stood on the break of the deck, a few feet from him, and a little raised, so as to have a good swing at him, and held in his hand the end of a thick, strong rope. The officers stood round, and the crew grouped together in the waist.
15 All these preparations made me feel sick and almost faint, angry and excited as I was. A man—a human being, made in God's likeness—fastened up and flogged like a beast! A man, too, whom I had lived with, eaten with, and stood watch with for months, and knew so well!

20 The first impulse was to resist—but what was to be done? Two men were fast, and there were left only two men besides Stimson and myself, and a small boy of ten or twelve years of age; and

Stimson and I would not have joined the men in a mutiny, as they knew. And then, on the other side, there were (besides the captain) three officers, steward, agent, and clerk, and the cabin supplied with weapons. But besides the numbers, what is there for sailors to do? If they resist, it is mutiny; and if they succeed, and take the vessel, it is piracy. If they ever yield again, their punishment must come; and if they do not yield, what are they to be for the rest of their lives? If a sailor resist his commander, he resists the law, and piracy or submission is his only alternative. Bad as it was, they saw it must be borne. It is what a sailor ships for. Swinging the rope over his head, and bending his body so as to give it full force, the captain brought it down upon the poor fellow's back. Once, twice,—six times. "Will you ever give me any more of your jaw?" The man writhed with pain, but said not a word. Three times more. This was too much, and he muttered something which I could not hear; this brought as many more as the man could stand, when the captain ordered him to be cut down.

"Now for you," said the captain, making up to John, and taking his irons off. As soon as John was loose, he ran forward to the forecastle. "Bring that man aft!" shouted the captain. The second mate, who had been in the forecastle with these men the early part of the voyage, stood still in the waist, and the mate walked slowly forward; but our third officer, anxious to show his zeal, sprang forward over the windlass, and laid hold of John; but John soon threw him from him. The captain stood on the quarter-deck, bareheaded, his eyes flashing with rage, and his face as red as blood, swinging the rope, and calling out to his officers, "Drag him aft! Lay hold of him! I'll *sweeten him!*" etc., etc. The mate now went forward, and told John quietly to go aft; and he, seeing resistance vain, threw the blackguard third mate from him, said he would go aft of himself, that they should not drag him, and went up to the gangway and held out his hands; but as soon as the captain began to make him fast, the indignity was too much, and he struggled; but, the mate and Russell holding him, he was soon seized up. When he was made fast, he turned to the captain, who stood rolling up his sleeves, getting ready for the blow, and asked him what he was to be flogged for. "Have I ever refused my duty, sir? Have you ever known me to hang back or to be insolent, or not to know my work?"

"No," said the captain, "it is not that that I flog you for; I flog you for your interference, for asking questions."

"Can't a man ask a question here without being flogged?"

"No," shouted the captain; "nobody shall open his mouth aboard this vessel but myself"; and he began laying the blows upon his back, swinging half round between each blow, to give it full effect. As he went on his passion increased, and he danced about the deck, calling out, as he swung the rope, "If you want to know what I flog you for, I'll tell you. It's because I like to do it! because I like to do it! It suits me! That's what I do it for!"

Exercise 9.1: Close Reading

In the blank space, write the *letter* of the choice that best completes the statement or answers the question.

1. The one who shows himself MOST lacking in self-control is _____.

    (A) the captain
    (B) John
    (C) Sam
    (D) the narrator

2. John does NOT put up a struggle when _____.

    (A) his irons are removed
    (B) he is put in irons
    (C) the captain orders him to be brought aft
    (D) the third mate lays hold of him

3. Which of the following happens first? _____

    (A) Sam is flogged.
    (B) John is flogged.
    (C) The third mate is thrown down.
    (D) John is put in irons.

4. The narrator does NOT try to stop the flogging because he feels _____.

    (A) it is none of his business
    (B) the captain should always be obeyed
    (C) all the odds are against him
    (D) Sam and John should not have talked back

5. The selection indicates that _____.

    (A) no sailor could be deprived of freedom of speech
    (B) the captain was absolute master aboard his ship
    (C) none of the mates wanted to obey the captain
    (D) the courts would have pardoned the sailors if they had seized the ship

6. How many were aboard the *Pilgrim*? _____

    (A) 12
    (B) 14
    (C) 18
    (D) 21

7. Which of the following statements is UNTRUE? _____

(A) The reason for Sam's punishment is neither mentioned nor hinted at.
(B) The ship's weapons are stored in the cabin.
(C) The captain does not charge John with being disrespectful.
(D) The mates vary in their enthusiasm for carrying out the captain's orders.

8. Of the following, which would be the best title for the selection? _____

(A) The Lure of the Sea
(B) Mutiny on the *Pilgrim*
(C) The Law of the Sea
(D) Triumph Over Tyranny

LEARNING NEW WORDS

Line	Word	Meaning	Typical Use
31	**alternative** *(n.)* òl-'tər-nət-iv	choice between two things; one of the two (or more) things from which a choice is to be made; choice	An election in which there is only one candidate is unfair to the voters because it does not give them an *alternative*.
20	**impulse** *(n.)* 'im-ˌpəls	sudden arousing of the mind and spirit to do something; sudden inclination to act; urge	When the home team scored the winning goal in the final seconds, the fans gave in to an uncontrollable *impulse* to surge onto the field.
55	**indignity** *(n.)* in-'dig-nət-ē	act that offends a person's dignity or self-respect; insult; outrage	The arrested man protested that he was innocent and that it was an *indignity* for him to be searched and fingerprinted.
60	**insolent** *(adj.)* 'in(t)-sə-lənt	boldly rude; disrespectful; insulting	Frank later realized that he had been *insolent* when he told his aunt that she didn't know what she was talking about.
		(ant. **courteous, respectful***)*	The stranger who asked for directions was *courteous;* she thanked us for our help.
48	**rage** *(n.)* 'rāj	violent and uncontrollable anger; fury	In a *rage* over not getting his way, Dale overturned his chair and ran out of the house, slamming the front door.

20	**resist** *(v.)*	exert force in opposition; fight against; oppose	The surrounded suspect gave himself up when he saw that it would be futile to *resist*.
	ri-'zist	*(ant.* **submit, yield**)	Instead of surrendering, the rebels swore that they would never *submit*.
31	**submission** *(n.)*	act of *submitting* (giving in or surrendering) to the power or authority of another; obedience	The invaders expected quick *submission* from the inhabitants, but they met with fierce resistance.
	səb-'mish-ən	*(ant.* **resistance**)	When the detective approached, the suspect surrendered quietly, without offering any *resistance*.
36	**writhe** *(v.)*	twist and turn this way and that; squirm	I couldn't sit still because my itching sunburn made me *writhe* in pain.
	'rīth		
29	**yield** *(v.)*	give up; cease resistance; surrender	The police called on the suspects to surrender but they refused to *yield*.
	'yēld	*(ant.* **resist**)	
46	**zeal** *(n.)*	active enthusiastic interest; eagerness; ardor; fervor	I used to do my piano practice with *zeal;* now I have little enthusiasm for it.
	'zēl	*(ant.* **apathy**)	If you were really interested in the club, you would come to meetings. By staying away, you are showing your *apathy*.

APPLYING WHAT YOU HAVE LEARNED

Exercise 9.2: Sentence Completion

Which of the two choices correctly completes the sentence? Write the *letter* of your answer in the space provided.

1. A person in a rage is _____.

    A. in a good mood   B. likely to be violent

2. My zeal for the subject has led me to do _____ is required.

    A. much more than   B. less than

3. _____ if you stop writhing.

    A. People will think you are lazy   B. The barber may be able to cut your hair

4. It is an indignity to _____.

    A. have a door slammed in your face   B. be praised for your work

5. Should we resist or _____?

    A. continue the fight   B. give in

6. When someone is insolent to you, he or she _____.

    A. is showing disrespect   B. does not mean to hurt your feelings

7. People who buy on impulse _____.

    A. never use cash   B. give little thought to what they are buying

8. The enemy yielded and _____.

    A. laid down their arms   B. called on us to surrender

9. When you have no alternative, you have _____.

    A. very few choices   B. no choice

10. The bandits' submission came as a surprise. No one believed they would ever _____.

    A. give up   B. get away

Exercise 9.3: Definitions

Each expression below defines a word taught on pages 118–119. Enter that word in the space provided.

_____ **1.** fight against

_____ **2.** act that offends a person's self-respect

_____ **3.** violent and uncontrollable anger

_____ **4.** sudden inclination to act

_____ **5.** give up

_____ **6.** choice between two things

_____ **7.** act of giving in to the power of another

_____ **8.** active enthusiastic interest

_____ **9.** boldly rude

_____ **10.** twist and turn this way and that

Exercise 9.4: Synonyms and Antonyms

A. Replace the italicized word with a *synonym* from the vocabulary list below.

_____ 1. My itching sunburn made me *squirm.*

_____ 2. She was in a *fury.*

_____ 3. Do you have any *choice*?

_____ 4. At that moment I had an *urge* to walk out.

_____ 5. Why does he think it an *outrage* to have to work?

B. Replace the italicized word with an *antonym* from the vocabulary list.

_____ 6. Their *resistance* came as no surprise.

_____ 7. Marie's brother was extremely *courteous.*

_____ 8. We thought they would not *resist.*

_____ 9. Fred worked on his report with *apathy.*

_____ 10. Circumstances compelled us to *submit.*

Vocabulary List

insolent	rage
indignity	yield
writhe	impulse
zeal	submission
resist	alternative

LEARNING SOME ROOTS AND DERIVATIVES

Each word in bold type is a **root**. The words below it are its **derivatives**.

alternate *(adj.)*	One way to get to the gym is by the elevator; an *alternate* way is by the stairs.
alternate *(v.)*	My brother and I *alternate* in cleaning our room; he cleans up one week, and I the next.
alternately *(adv.)*	We clean our room *alternately.*
alternative *(n.)*	Since the elevator was not running, the only way for us to get to the gym was by the stairs; we had no *alternative.*

impulse *(n.)*	When Gordon thinks he knows the answer, he cannot resist the *impulse* to blurt it out.
impulsive *(adj.)*	Instead of being *impulsive,* Gordon should get permission before he speaks.
impulsively *(adv.)*	He is bound to be disliked if he continues to answer *impulsively.*
insolent *(adj.)*	You were *insolent* to my friend when you told her to mind her own business.
insolently *(adv.)*	She was not rude to you. Why did you speak so *insolently* to her?
insolence *(n.)*	You can accomplish more through courtesy than through *insolence.*
rage *(n.)*	When the dictator heard that his orders had not been carried out, he was in a *rage.*
rage *(v.)*	He *raged* like a madman.
resist *(v.)*	Proper rest, diet, and exercise will help you *resist* disease.
resistant *(adj.)*	A healthy body is usually *resistant* to disease.
resistance *(n.)*	Your physician can help you build up your *resistance.*
submit *(v.)*	The Boston patriots refused to *submit* to King George.
submissive *(adj.)*	They were not *submissive.*
submissively *(adv.)*	They would not *submissively* obey the commands of a foreign ruler.
submission *(n.)*	They refused to pay the tax on tea because to do so would have been an act of *submission.*
zeal *(n.)*	Martha is supporting me with remarkable *zeal;* she has persuaded several of her friends to vote for me.
zealous *(adj.)*	Martha is one of my most *zealous* supporters.
zealously *(adv.)*	Martha is *zealously* working for my election.

Exercise 9.5: Roots and Derivatives

Fill each blank below with the root or derivative just listed that best completes the sentence.

1. Don't _____ like a madman! Control your anger!

2. I guess I must have acted _____. I don't know what made me walk out.

3. Some _____ baseball fans travel to Florida to watch their favorite teams in spring exhibition games.

4. There was some construction work on the highway; therefore, we took a(n) _____ route.

5. The colt at first was not _____, throwing anyone who ventured to ride him.

6. Their rudeness to our visitors was unpardonable. We were deeply embarrassed by their _____.

7. A(n) _____ person is one who acts on a sudden inclination, without bothering to think of the consequences.

8. Barbara, one of our very eager new members, acted as secretary, and she took the minutes _____.

9. The team on the court was rude when we asked them for a chance to play; they _____ told us to "get lost."

10. Some of the rebels did not submit, but fled to the hills to continue their _____.

IMPROVING YOUR SPELLING: WORDS ENDING IN -ANCE, -ENCE, -ANT, AND -ENT

"... and he, seeing *resistance* vain ..."

"... I flog you for your *interference* ..."

1. Why do some nouns, like *resistance,* end in -ANCE, while others, like *interference,* end in -ENCE?

There is no simple rule to help with this problem. You must study each commonly used -ANCE and -ENCE noun separately, and consult the dictionary when in doubt. Here are some nouns to review.

-ANCE		-ENCE	
abundance	endurance	adherence	indifference
allegiance	extravagance	adolescence	indolence
appliance	ignorance	affluence	indulgence
assistance	importance	audience	insolence
attendance	observance	coherence	interference
brilliance	perseverance	confidence	negligence
compliance	reliance	correspondence	occurrence
defiance	repentance	impatience	permanence
disturbance	resemblance	incompetence	vehemence
elegance	resistance	independence	violence

2. (A) Note that many nouns ending in -ANCE become adjectives ending in -ANT.

ignorANCE   ignorANT
N   ADJ

(B) Certain -ANCE nouns, however, become adjectives by adding -ING, rather than -ANT.

endurANCE   endurING
N   ADJ

(C) Many nouns ending in -ENCE become adjectives ending in -ENT.

insolENCE   insolENT
N   ADJ

Exercise 9.6: Changing Nouns to Adjectives

The first change has been made as a sample.

NOUN	ADJECTIVE
1. independence	**independent**
2. brilliance	
3. abundance	
4. vehemence	
5. disturbance	
6. repentance	
7. indolence	
8. perseverance	
9. coherence	
10. reliance	

Exercise 9.7: Changing Adjectives to Nouns

The first change has been entered as a sample.

ADJECTIVE	NOUN
1. defiant	**defiance**
2. extravagant	
3. indifferent	
4. indulgent	
5. enduring	
6. permanent	
7. confident	

8. assistant   _____

9. ignorant   _____

10. resembling   _____

Exercise 9.8: Word Completion

Write the missing letter in column A and the complete word in column B.

Column A   *Column B*

1. repent __ nt   _____

2. compli __ nce   _____

3. indiffer __ nt   _____

4. adolesc __ nce   _____

5. self-confid __ nt   _____

6. persever __ nce   _____

7. incoher __ nt   _____

8. occurr __ nce   _____

9. appli __ nce   _____

10. eleg __ nt   _____

11. resist __ nce   _____

12. self-reli __ nt   _____

13. disturb __ nce   _____

14. vehem __ nt   _____

15. interfer __ nce   _____

16. unimport __ nt   _____

17. viol __ nce   _____

18. observ __ nt   _____

19. allegi __ nce   _____

20. adher __ nt   _____

PUNCTUATING WORDS OF DIRECT ADDRESS

1. Words of **direct address** are words that tell us to whom a remark is being directed.

   The italicized words below are words of direct address:

   When are you leaving , *Jennifer*?

   Bob , your breakfast is ready.

   I am here today , *my fellow students* , to ask for your support.

2. Set off words of direct address from the rest of the sentence by commas.

   Use *one* comma when words of direct address begin or end the sentence:

   Linda , please mail these letters on your way to school.

   Please mail these letters on your way to school , *Linda*.

   Otherwise, use *two* commas:

   Please mail these letters , *Linda* , on your way to school.

Exercise 9.9: Using Required Punctuation
Rewrite each sentence, adding the necessary punctuation.

1. Wait for me Joe

   _____

2. What are you going to flog that man for sir

   _____

3. Dad this call is for you

   _____

4. Are you feeling better Jack

   _____

5. Listen my children and you shall hear

   _____

6. Norman please close the window

   _____

7. May I ask a question Mr. Carr

   _____

8. This ladies and gentlemen is our last chance

_____

9. Pat is this yours

_____

10. Have I ever refused my duty sir

_____

IMPROVING YOUR COMPOSITION SKILLS: BEGINNING A PARAGRAPH WITH A QUESTION

Richard Henry Dana, Jr., distressed that a man he had eaten with and stood watch with is about to be flogged like a beast, begins a paragraph with this question (page 114, line 20):

"The first impulse was to resist—but what was to be done?"

Then, he proceeds to answer that question and to give reasons for his answer.

Exercise 9.10: Writing a Paragraph Beginning With a Question

In your first sentence, ask a question. In the rest of the paragraph, answer that question and give reasons for your answer. Write about a hundred words.

Hints for the first sentence:

How should we deal with litterbugs?
Should Americans buy foreign cars?
Who are the worst polluters?
Should the school year be lengthened?
What should be done about drunken drivers?
Should our states run lotteries?

Sample Paragraph Beginning With a Question

> **Should our states run lotteries? I think not. A lottery is immoral. It is like stealing because it takes people's money and offers them only the tiniest of chances of winning the jackpot. It encourages the false belief that success in life can come through luck only, and that saving and hard work have nothing to do with it. It is especially cruel to the poor who spend millions and millions of their hard-earned wages each day on lottery tickets—instead of on food, clothing, medical attention, and other necessities for their families.**

Comment: The first sentence asks a question. The second answers it. The rest of the paragraph supports that answer with reasons.

Now write your paragraph beginning with a question.

_____

_____

_____

_____

_____

_____

_____

_____

_____

_____

_____

Old Yeller

by Fred Gipson

In an emergency, do you lose your head, or do you remain calm enough to act intelligently?

The narrator, a fourteen-year-old boy living in the Texas hill country in the 1860's, describes an emergency in which he was involved.

That's when I heard Little Arliss scream.

Well, Little Arliss was a screamer by nature. He'd scream when he was happy and scream when he was mad and a lot of times he'd scream just to hear himself make a noise. Generally,
5 we paid no more mind to his screaming than we did to the gobble of a wild turkey.

But this time was different. The second I heard his screaming, I felt my heart flop clear over. This time I knew Little Arliss was in real trouble.

10 I tore out up the trail leading toward the cabin. A minute before, I'd been so tired out with my rail splitting that I couldn't have struck a trot. But now I raced through the tall trees in that creek bottom, covering ground like a scared wolf.

Little Arliss's second scream, when it came, was louder and
15 shriller and more frantic-sounding than the first. Mixed with it was a whimpering crying sound that I knew didn't come from him. It was a sound I'd heard before and seemed like I ought to know what it was, but right then I couldn't place it.

Then, from way off to one side came a sound that I would have
20 recognized anywhere. It was the coughing roar of a charging bear. I'd just heard it once in my life. That was the time Mama had shot

and wounded a hog-killing bear and Papa had had to finish it off with a knife to keep it from getting her.

My heart went to pushing up into my throat, nearly choking off my wind. I strained for every lick of speed I could get out of my running legs. I didn't know what sort of fix Little Arliss had got himself into, but I knew that it had to do with a mad bear, which was enough.

The way the late sun slanted through the trees had the trail all cross-banded with streaks of bright light and dark shade. I ran through these bright and dark patches so fast that the changing light nearly blinded me. Then suddenly, I raced out into the open where I could see ahead. And what I saw sent a chill clear through to the marrow of my bones.

There was Little Arliss, down in that spring hole again. He was lying half in and half out of the water, holding onto the hind leg of a little black bear cub no bigger than a small coon. The bear cub was out on the bank, whimpering and crying and clawing the rocks with all three of his other feet, trying to pull away. But Little Arliss was holding on for all he was worth, scared now and screaming his head off. Too scared to let go.

How come the bear cub ever got to prowl close enough for Little Arliss to grab him, I don't know. And why he didn't turn on him and bite loose, I couldn't figure out, either. Unless he was like Little Arliss, too scared to think.

But all of that didn't matter now. What mattered was the bear cub's mama. She'd heard the cries of her baby and was coming to save him. She was coming so fast that she had the brush popping and breaking as she crashed through and over it. I could see her black heavy figure piling off down the slant on the far side of Bird-song Creek. She was roaring mad and ready to kill.

And worst of all, I could see that I'd never get there in time!

Mama couldn't either. She'd heard Arliss, too, and here she came from the cabin, running down the slant toward the spring, screaming at Arliss, telling him to turn the bear cub loose. But Little Arliss wouldn't do it. All he'd do was hang with that hind leg and let out one shrill shriek after another as fast as he could suck in a breath.

Now the she bear was charging across the shallows in the creek. She was knocking sheets of water high in the bright sun, charging with her fur up and her long teeth bared, filling the canyon with that awful coughing roar. And no matter how fast Mama ran or how fast I ran, the she bear was going to get there first!

I think I nearly went blind then, picturing what was going to happen to Little Arliss. I know that I opened my mouth to scream and not any sound came out.

Then, just as the bear went lunging up the creek bank toward Little Arliss and her cub, a flash of yellow came streaking out of the brush.

It was that big yeller dog. He was roaring like a mad bull. He wasn't one-third as big and heavy as the she bear, but when he

piled into her from one side, he rolled her clear off her feet. They
went down in a wild, roaring tangle of twisting bodies and scram-
75 bling feet and slashing fangs.

As I raced past them, I saw the bear lunge up to stand on her
hind feet like a man while she clawed at the body of the yeller dog
hanging to her throat. I didn't wait to see more. Without ever
checking my stride, I ran in and jerked Little Arliss loose from the
80 cub. I grabbed him by the wrist and yanked him up out of that
water and slung him toward Mama like he was a half-empty sack
of corn. I screamed at Mama. "Grab him, Mama! Grab him and
run!" Then I swung my chopping axe high and wheeled, aiming
to cave in the she bear's head with the first lick.

Line 37. *coon:* raccoon

UNDERSTANDING THE SELECTION

Exercise 10.1: Close Reading

In the blank space, write the *letter* of the choice that best completes the statement or
answers the question.

1. The whimpering and crying sound came from _____ .

   (A) Little Arliss
   (B) a mad she bear
   (C) a bear cub
   (D) a raccoon

2. According to the narrator, Arliss kept holding on to the cub because _____ .

   (A) he was frightened
   (B) he didn't want it to escape
   (C) it had a grip on him
   (D) he didn't want it to bite him

3. The selection compares _____ to a mad bull.

   (A) Arliss
   (B) the bear
   (C) the bear cub
   (D) the yellow dog

4. The main incident described in the selection occurred at about _____ .

   (A) noon
   (B) 5 P.M.
   (C) 11 A.M.
   (D) 8 A.M.

5. The selection suggests that _____.

    (A) bear cubs are harmless
    (B) Papa is not at home
    (C) Mama handles a rifle expertly
    (D) there is little game in the area

6. The narrator's attitude toward the she-bear is LEAST sympathetic in _____.

    (A) lines 26–28
    (B) lines 46–48
    (C) lines 60–62
    (D) lines 83–84

7. As he rushed toward the cabin, the narrator was _____.

    (A) carrying a rifle
    (B) armed with a knife
    (C) unarmed
    (D) carrying an axe

8. Which of the following would be the best title for the selection? _____

    (A) A Scream and a Whimper
    (B) Panic
    (C) A Race Against Time
    (D) A Flash of Yellow

LEARNING NEW WORDS

Line	Word	Meaning	Typical Use
70	**brush** (*n.*) 'brəsh	thick growth of bushes, shrubs, and small trees; brushwood; scrub	The forest rangers had to cut their way through the *brush* to reach the scene of the crash.
79	**check** (*v.*) 'chek	bring to a sudden halt; stop; restrain; curb	Decay in a tooth must be *checked* as soon as it is discovered.
37	**cub** (*n.*) 'kəb	1. young bear, lion, or fox	The lioness and her mate take care of their *cubs* until they can fend for themselves.
		2. apprentice, especially an inexperienced newspaper reporter; novice; beginner	Students without previous experience are assigned as *cubs* when they join the staff of the school newspaper.

75	**fang** (n.) 'faŋ	long, sharp, pointed tooth by which an animal's prey is seized and held or torn; tooth	Anyone whose skin is pierced by the *fangs* of a poisonous snake must receive first aid immediately.
15	**frantic** (adj.) 'frant-ik	wildly or uncontrollably excited; frenzied	The *frantic* tenants would have leaped from the roof if the rescuers had not reached them in time.
4	**generally** (adv.) 'jen-(ə-)rə-lē	usually; as a rule; in most cases	*Generally*, my sister picks up the phone when it rings, but this time I got to it first.
76	**lunge** (v.) 'lənj	make a sudden forceful movement; plunge	One of our guards *lunged* at the swift ball carrier but failed to tackle him.
34	**marrow** (n.) 'mar-ō	soft tissue that fills the cavities of most bones; inmost, best, or essential part	It was so cold in the room that I was chilled to the *marrow* of my bones.
42	**prowl** (v.) 'praúl	move about slowly and stealthily like a wild beast seeking prey; lurk; roam in search of whatever may be found	The residents feared that the escaped tiger might be *prowling* near their homes.
16	**whimper** (v.) 'hwim-pər	cry with low, complaining, broken sounds; whine	The child did not cry loudly but *whimpered* for nearly half an hour before falling asleep.

APPLYING WHAT YOU HAVE LEARNED

Exercise 10.2: Sentence Completion

Which of the two choices correctly completes the sentence? Write the *letter* of your answer in the space provided.

1. Were you frantic when you were in danger or did you _____?

    A. get excited   B. remain calm

2. When the coach says "Lunge," everyone is to _____.

    A. move forward forcefully   B. step aside gently

3. Visitors to the zoo often pay more attention to the cubs than to the ____ animals.

    A. younger   B. older

4. We must check the Red Sox rally to ____.

    A. see if errors were made   B. prevent further scoring

5. When the lion bared his fangs, I could see what sharp ____ he has.

    A. claws   B. teeth

6. Stop whimpering. You have nothing to ____ about.

    A. cry   B. brag

7. A ____ would have little trouble getting through the brush.

    A. wagon   B. snake

8. Inside the ____ is a substance called the marrow.

    A. bone   B. branch

9. Stan is generally on time; he is ____ late.

    A. never   B. seldom

10. If you see someone prowling in the neighborhood, it may be ____.

    A. a burglar   B. the postman

Exercise 10.3: Definitions

Each expression below defines a word taught on pages 132–133. Enter that word in the space provided.

_____ **1.** wildly or uncontrollably excited

_____ **2.** make a forceful forward movement

_____ **3.** long, sharp, pointed tooth

_____ **4.** cry with low, complaining, broken sounds

_____ **5.** as a rule

_____ **6.** young bear, lion, or fox

_____ **7.** soft tissue that fills bone cavities

_____ **8.** move about slowly and stealthily

_____ **9.** bring to a sudden halt

_____ **10.** thick growth of bushes, shrubs, and small trees

Exercise 10.4: Synonyms

In the space before each word or expression in column A, write its synonym selected from column B.

	Column A	*Column B*
_____	**1.** frenzied	cub
_____	**2.** whine	lunge
_____	**3.** usually	check
_____	**4.** novice	whimper
_____	**5.** inmost part	prowl
_____	**6.** scrub	marrow
_____	**7.** stop	frantic
_____	**8.** tooth	brush
_____	**9.** plunge	fang
_____	**10.** lurk	generally

LEARNING SOME ROOTS AND DERIVATIVES

Each word in bold type is a **root**. The words below it are its **derivatives**.

brush *(n.)*   It is much easier to spot a golf ball in the short grass than one that has rolled into the *brush*.

brushwood *(n.)*   We have enough logs for the fire, but we could use some pieces of *brushwood* for kindling.

check *(v.)*   A way must be found to *check* unemployment.

check *(n.)*   A road-building program will create jobs and serve as a *check* to unemployment.

unchecked *(adj.)*   Unemployment must not be permitted to continue *unchecked*.

frantic *(adj.)*   As I approached the water, I heard a *frantic* cry for help.

frantically *(adv.)*   Someone whose boat had overturned was shouting *frantically* for help.

general *(adj.)*	The dean's *general* practice is to notify your parents if you get into trouble.
generally *(adv.)*	*Generally,* the dean will notify your parents if you get into trouble.
lunge *(v.)*	The challenger *lunged* at Jackson with a powerful right, but missed.
lunge *(n.)*	Luckily, Jackson avoided the *lunge.*
marrow *(n.)*	The bones of our arms and legs are filled with *marrow.*
marrowy *(adj.)*	Red blood cells are produced in the *marrowy* tissues of our bones.
prowl *(v.)*	Stray cats *prowl* the streets at night.
prowl *(n.)*	Our garbage can was knocked over by a stray dog on the *prowl.*
prowler *(n.)*	The neighbor's cat stays indoors; he is no *prowler.*
whimper *(v.)*	Mother got up when she heard the baby *whimper.*
whimper *(n.)*	Mother was awakened by the baby's *whimper.*

Exercise 10.5: Roots and Derivatives

Fill each blank with the root or derivative just listed that best completes the sentence.

1. Our neighbor called the police at 2 A.M. when he thought he saw a(n) _____ in the back yard.

2. Alex, who was uncontrollably excited by the decision, argued with the umpires so _____ that he was thrown out of the game.

3. The chef says that _____ bones are good for soup.

4. We will be able to make quicker progress once we get out of the _____ and into the open fields.

5. For years we permitted our air and water to be polluted without even a(n) _____ of protest.

6. *Theater* is now the _____ spelling; *theatre* is becoming more and more rare.

7. In fencing, when you make a(n) _____ at your opponent, you suddenly extend your right arm and advance your right foot as far as possible.

8. If a forest fire is allowed to rage _____, it will spread very rapidly.

9. Two detectives followed the suspect as he began his nightly _____.

10. The Supreme Court exercises a(n) _____ on the misuse of power by legislators when it declares a law unconstitutional.

The passage we have just read from *Old Yeller* contains a large number of the words appearing in the famous list of *One Hundred Spelling Demons* below. These words are so often used that everyone should be able to spell them with complete accuracy.

Review the list. Then do the exercise that follows.

One Hundred Spelling Demons

ache	done	making	they
again	don't	many	though
always	early	meant	through
among	easy	minute	tired
answer	enough	much	tonight
any	every	none	too
been	February	often	trouble
beginning	forty	once	truly
believe	friend	piece	Tuesday
blue	grammar	raise	two
break	guess	read	used
built	half	ready	very
business	having	said	wear
busy	hear	says	Wednesday
buy	heard	seems	week
can't	here	separate	where
choose	hoarse	shoes	whether
color	hour	since	which
coming	instead	some	whole
cough	just	straight	women
could	knew	sugar	won't
country	know	sure	would
dear	laid	tear	write
doctor	loose	their	writing
does	lose	there	wrote

Exercise 10.6: Word Completion

Insert the missing letters and write the complete word.

1. **T __ __ p __ __ ces** of pie should be **en __ __ gh.**

   _____   _____   _____

2. **I bel __ __ ve the ans __ __ r** is **f __ rty-four.**

   _____   _____   _____

3. My **fr _ _ nd** Pat has no **tr _ _ ble** with her **gramm _ r.**

_____ _____ _____

4. Many **w _ men w _ _ r** high-heeled **sh _ _ s.**

_____ _____ _____

5. My voice is **h _ _ rse, Doct _ r,** and I have a bad **c _ _ gh.**

_____ _____ _____

6. She **s _ _ d** she'd be **r _ _ dy** in a **min _ _ _ .**

_____ _____ _____

7. It snowed the last **T _ _ sday** and **We _ _ _ _ sday** in **Feb _ _ ary.**

_____ _____ _____

8. In the **c _ _ ntry,** the leaves are **beg _ _ _ ing** to change **c _ l _ r.**

_____ _____ _____

9. Noisy sanitation trucks rumble **thr _ _ gh** town at an _ _ **rly h _ _ r.**

_____ _____ _____

10. Ask the waiter **w _ _ _ ther** he can seat us together, **inst _ _ d** of **sep _ rately.**

_____ _____ _____

INTRODUCING THE PRESENT PARTICIPLE

A knowledge of the **present participle** can help you become a better writer. First let us show you how to form the present participle. Then we will explain what the present participle does and how you can use it.

To form the present participle of a verb, add **ing:**

> whimper + ing = whimpering
> charge + ing = charging
> run + ing = running

Exercise 10.7: Forming Present Participles

Below are some verbs that Fred Gipson uses in *Old Yeller.* What is the present participle of each of these verbs? The first participle has been entered as a sample.

Verb	Present Participle
1. cover	**covering**
2. choke	_____
3. hold	_____

4. cry   _____

5. claw   _____

6. pop   _____

7. charge   _____

8. picture   _____

9. lunge   _____

10. aim   _____

IMPROVING YOUR COMPOSITION SKILLS: USING PRESENT PARTICIPLES

Question: Which of the following is a better description? Why?

Description A

> She came from the cabin. She ran down the slant toward the spring. She screamed at Arliss. She told him to turn the bear cub loose.

Description B

> She came from the cabin, **running** down the slant toward the spring, **screaming** at Arliss, **telling** him to turn the bear cub loose.

Answer: Description B is superior because—by using the present participles *running, screaming, telling*—it achieves these advantages:

1. It avoids unnecessary repetition of the subject *she. She* is used four times in Description A, but only once in Description B.

2. It replaces the four choppy sentences in Description A with a smoother, faster-moving sentence.

3. It makes the description more exciting and more interesting.

Punctuation Note: Use a comma to set off the participial phrase from the rest of the sentence. Study these examples:

    (a) I left the room, *taking my books.*

    (b) *Taking my books,* I left the room.

Exercise 10.8: Using Present Participles to Combine Sentences

Improve each group of sentences below by combining them into one sentence, as in the following sample:

> SAMPLE: They passed us quickly. They looked angry.
> **They passed us quickly, looking angry.**

1. We talked for a while. We exchanged ideas.

   _____

2. Fred drove by on his motorbike. He waved to his friends.

   _____

3. I raced through the tall trees in that creek bottom. I covered ground like a scared wolf.

   _____

   _____

4. The river overflowed. It flooded streets and basements.

   _____

5. The bear cub was out on the bank. He whimpered. He cried. He clawed the rocks. He tried to pull away.

   _____

   _____

6. A woman with a tall hat sat directly in front of me. She blocked my view.

   _____

   _____

7. He was lying half in and half out of the water. He was holding on to the hind leg of a little black bear cub.

   _____

   _____

8. They started at 8 A.M. They hoped to finish by noon.

   _____

9. I entered quickly. I left the door behind me open.

   _____

10. A thick fog settled on the Eastern Seaboard. It reduced visibility. It shut down most of the airports. It snarled traffic on the highways.

   _____

   _____

An Occurrence at Owl Creek Bridge

by Ambrose Bierce

The following takes place in the center of a railroad bridge over a stream in Northern Alabama during the Civil War.

The man who was engaged in being hanged was apparently about thirty-five years of age. He was a civilian, if one might judge from his habit, which was that of a planter. His features were good—a straight nose, firm mouth, broad forehead, from which his
5   long, dark hair was combed straight back, falling behind his ears to the collar of his well-fitting frock coat. He wore a mustache and pointed beard, but no whiskers; his eyes were large and dark gray, and had a kindly expression which one would hardly have expected in one whose neck was in the hemp. Evidently this was
10 no vulgar assassin. The liberal military code makes provision for hanging many kinds of persons, and gentlemen are not excluded.

The preparations being complete, the two private soldiers stepped aside and each drew away the plank upon which he had been standing. The sergeant turned to the captain, saluted and
15 placed himself immediately behind that officer, who in turn moved apart one pace. These movements left the condemned man and the sergeant standing on the two ends of the same plank, which spanned three of the cross-ties of the bridge. The end upon which the civilian stood almost, but not quite, reached a fourth. This
20 plank had been held in place by the weight of the captain; it was now held by that of the sergeant. At a signal from the former the latter would step aside, the plank would tilt and the condemned man go down between two ties. The arrangement commended itself to his judgment as simple and effective. His face had not

been covered nor his eyes bandaged. He looked a moment at his "unsteadfast footing," then let his gaze wander to the swirling water of the stream racing madly beneath his feet. A piece of dancing driftwood caught his attention and his eyes followed it down the current. How slowly it appeared to move! What a sluggish stream!

He closed his eyes in order to fix his last thoughts upon his wife and children. The water, touched to gold by the early sun, the brooding mists under the banks at some distance down the stream, the fort, the soldiers, the piece of drift—all had distracted him. And now he became conscious of a new disturbance. Striking through the thought of his dear ones was a sound which he could neither ignore nor understand, a sharp, distinct, metallic percussion like the stroke of a blacksmith's hammer upon the anvil; it had the same ringing quality. He wondered what it was, and whether immeasurably distant or near by—it seemed both. Its recurrence was regular, but as slow as the tolling of a death knell. He waited each stroke with impatience and—he knew not why— apprehension. The intervals of silence grew progressively longer; the delays became maddening. With their greater infrequency the sounds increased in strength and sharpness. They hurt his ear like the thrust of a knife; he feared he would shriek. What he heard was the ticking of his watch.

He unclosed his eyes and saw again the water below him. "If I could free my hands," he thought, "I might throw off the noose and spring into the stream. By diving I could evade the bullets and, swimming vigorously, reach the bank, take to the woods and get away home. My home, thank God, is as yet outside their lines; my wife and little ones are still beyond the invader's farthest advance."

Line 18. *cross-ties:* timbers across which railroad rails are fastened

UNDERSTANDING THE SELECTION

Exercise 11.1: Close Reading

In the blank space, write the *letter* of the choice that best completes the statement or answers the question.

1. The action described in the selection takes place _____.

   (A) before sunrise
   (B) at sundown
   (C) in the early morning
   (D) in the late afternoon

2. The plank on which the condemned man is standing is being held in place by _____.

   (A) three cross-ties
   (B) the weight of two private soldiers
   (C) two other planks
   (D) the weight of the sergeant

3. The selection suggests that _____.

   (A) there is a fort nearby
   (B) the condemned man's hands are loosely tied
   (C) there are no armed soldiers at the scene
   (D) the condemned man is a common criminal

4. The condemned man _____.

   (A) imagines that time is slipping away altogether too rapidly
   (B) has given up all hope of escape
   (C) does not understand that his watch is making unbearably painful sounds
   (D) imagines that his home has been destroyed by the enemy

5. The author is mainly concerned with describing _____.

   (A) the setting
   (B) what is happening in the mind of the condemned man
   (C) the thoughts of the officers and soldiers
   (D) the appearance of the condemned man

6. The selection neither states nor suggests that the condemned man is a(n) _____.

   (A) parent
   (B) swimmer
   (C) assassin
   (D) bachelor

7. Which of the following words is used in a way that is directly the OPPOSITE of its usual meaning? _____

   (A) liberal (line 10)
   (B) gentlemen (line 11)
   (C) simple (line 24)
   (D) effective (line 24)

8. Which of the following would make the best title for the selection? _____

   (A) Mistaken Identity
   (B) A Narrow Escape
   (C) Military Justice
   (D) Behind Enemy Lines

Line	Word	Meaning	Typical Use
1	**apparently** *(adv.)* ə-'par-ənt-lē	1. in an *apparent* (plain to see or visible) manner; evidently; obviously	Milly is *apparently* angry with me, as she hasn't said anything to me in a long time.
		2. seemingly (but not necessarily really)	The *apparently* worthless nag that Billy Dawes led past the British guards was one of the fastest horses in Boston.
		(*ant.* **really**)	
43	**apprehension** *(n.)* ˌap-ri-'hen-chən	fear of what may be coming; dread	Since I had reviewed my notes carefully, I took the test without *apprehension*.
		(*ant.* **confidence**)	As I was well prepared, I took the test with a feeling of *confidence*.
34	**distract** *(v.)* dis-'trakt	draw away (the attention or mind) to a different subject; divert	While the bus is in motion, do not do or say anything to *distract* the driver's attention.
50	**evade** *(v.)* i-'vād	1. get away from or avoid by skill or cleverness; elude	The candidate *evaded* the reporters by slipping out through a back door.
		2. avoid facing up to	Answer truthfully; do not attempt to *evade* the question.
11	**exclude** *(v.)* iks-'klüd	shut out; keep out; bar from participation or inclusion	The security force is under instructions to *exclude* anyone who cannot show proper identification.
		(*ant.* **admit**)	Employees not wearing an identification badge will not be *admitted* at the gate.
		(*ant.* **include**)	The price *includes* postage and handling, but not local sales taxes.
21	**former** *(adj.)* 'för-mər	coming before in time; earlier; previous; prior	Gloria feels better; she is beginning to recover her *former* strength.
	(n.)	first of two	Ralph and Bob are fine athletes. The *former* is our best

			pitcher. The *latter* is on the track team.
37	**ignore** *(v.)* ig-'nô(ə)r	refuse to take notice of; disregard	The accident occurred when one of the drivers *ignored* a red light.
	(ant. **heed**)		If he had *heeded* the traffic signal, the accident would have been prevented.
22	**latter** *(adj.)* 'lat-ər	more recent; later	Computers came into use in the *latter* half of the twentieth century.
	(n.)	second of two *(ant.* **former**)	Both Lincoln and Washington were born in February—the *former* on the twelfth, and the *latter* on the twenty-second.
41	**recurrence** *(n.)* ri-'kər-ən(t)s	act of *recurring* (occurring or happening again); repetition	After a serious accident at this intersection, steps were taken to prevent a *recurrence*.
22	**tilt** *(v.)* 'tilt	cause to slope; incline; tip; slant	Since both teams are evenly matched, an injury to one of our key players can *tilt* the scales in favor of our opponents.

APPLYING WHAT YOU HAVE LEARNED

Exercise 11.2: Sentence Completion

Which of the two choices correctly completes the sentence? Write the *letter* of your answer in the space provided.

1. You can go west by rail or by air, but the latter is usually _____.

    A. slower   B. faster

2. They tried to get _____, but they were excluded.

    A. out   B. in

3. Alice ignored us; she _____.

    A. asked us a great number of questions   B. pretended that we didn't even exist

4. If you sit _____ of that long bench, it may tilt.

    A. at the end   B. in the middle

5. A painting described as an apparently original Picasso _____.

    A. is definitely the work of that artist   B. may be an imitation

6. I _____ of the announcement because Sam distracted me.

    A. did not miss a single word   B. missed part

7. Both Alaska and Rhode Island are states, though the former is much _____.

    A. smaller   B. larger

8. _____ his first failure in spelling, Stan assured his parents that there would be no recurrence.

    A. Before   B. After

9. Our puppy ran _____ the postman, as if to evade him.

    A. after   B. away from

10. My aunt expressed apprehension about the trip because _____.

    A. she needed a vacation   B. the roads were slippery

Exercise 11.3: Definitions

Each expression below defines a word taught on pages 144–145. Enter that word in the space provided.

_____ **1.** draw away the attention

_____ **2.** act of happening again

_____ **3.** keep out

_____ **4.** second of two

_____ **5.** fear of what may be coming

_____ **6.** refuse to take notice of

_____ **7.** cause to slope

_____ **8.** in a plain-to-see manner

_____ **9.** avoid by skill or cleverness

_____ **10.** first of two

Exercise 11.4: Synonyms and Antonyms

A. Replace the italicized word with a *synonym* from the vocabulary list on the next page.

_____ **1.** Mike tried to *elude* us.

_____ **2.** There may be a *repetition* of last year's power failure.

_____ **3.** How can I do my work if you *divert* my attention?

_____ **4.** Don't *tip* the boat!

_____ **5.** Diane hoped for a return of her *previous* good luck.

B. Replace the italicized word with an *antonym* from the vocabulary list.

_____ **6.** I am sure they will *admit* us.

_____ **7.** In all probability, George will *heed* the warning.

_____ **8.** They chose the *former* of the two alternatives.

_____ **9.** She undertook the assignment with *confidence.*

_____ **10.** The magician *really* swallowed a sword.

Vocabulary List

distract	apparently
ignore	evade
former	latter
apprehension	tilt
recurrence	exclude

LEARNING SOME ROOTS AND DERIVATIVES

Each word in bold type is a **root**. The words below it are its **derivatives**.

apparent *(adj.)*	Your smile makes it *apparent* that you are pleased with your mark.
apparently *(adv.)*	*Apparently* you are pleased with your mark.
apprehend *(v.)*	There is no need to *apprehend* the outcome since everything will turn out all right.
apprehensive *(adj.)*	There is no reason to be *apprehensive.*
apprehensively *(adv.)*	Why do you look to the future *apprehensively*?
apprehension *(n.)*	Don't be afraid. I assure you that there is no cause for *apprehension.*
distract *(v.)*	I tried to study, but the loud playing of my neighbor's stereo *distracted* me.
distraction *(n.)*	My mother turns the TV off when I study to prevent it from being a *distraction.*
evade *(v.)*	The suspect *evaded* several questions by answering, "I can't remember."

evasive *(adj.)*	He gave *evasive* replies.
evasively *(adv.)*	He answered *evasively*.
evasion *(n.)*	He practiced *evasion*.
exclude *(v.)*	Tracy's Supermart has the right to *exclude* the cars of non-customers from its private parking lot.
exclusive *(adj.)*	The Tracy lot is for the *exclusive* use of Tracy shoppers.
exclusively *(adv.)*	Tracy's maintains a parking field *exclusively* for its own patrons.
exclusion *(n.)*	If not for the *exclusion* of the general public, Tracy's clients would be unable to park in Tracy's lot.
former *(adj.)*	My *former* favorite ice cream was strawberry.
former *(n.)*	When given a choice between strawberry and pistachio, I always took the *former*.
formerly *(adv.)*	*Formerly,* I used to avoid all flavors except strawberry.
latter *(adj.)*	In her former appearances, the actress was unnoticed, but in her *latter* roles she has won much praise.
latter *(n.)*	At first she appeared in small parts. Then she began getting major roles. The *latter* have given her an opportunity to become known.
latterly *(adv.)*	She had never been on television. *Latterly,* however, she has been a guest performer on numerous TV shows.
recur *(v.)*	Certain districts are plagued by floods that *recur* every spring.
recurrent *(adj.)*	The residents are annoyed by the *recurrent* floods.
recurrence *(n.)*	After each severe flood, they talk about what needs to be done to prevent a *recurrence*.
tilt *(v.)*	In going out, I brushed against the wall mirror, causing it to *tilt* slightly.
tilt *(n.)*	By moving the right side of the mirror up slightly, I corrected the *tilt*.

Exercise 11.5: Roots and Derivatives

Fill each blank below with the root or derivative just listed that best completes the sentence.

1. The pain is gone now, and I hope it will not _____.

2. From the way traffic was moving, it was _____ that our bus would not get to school on time.

3. The police have twice spotted their suspect in midtown but could not catch up with him; he is remarkably _____.

4. Coats that were _____ $150 are now on sale for $79.

5. The party is _____ for members of the Spanish Club; no one else will be invited.

6. There is a slight _____ in the furniture on one side of the room where the floor is uneven.

7. Her mother became _____ when she heard the baby's cough, and she immediately called the doctor.

8. The World Series is a powerful _____. It prevents people, especially baseball fans, from keeping their minds on their work.

9. Since last March there have been _____ power failures in our neighborhood, about one every two weeks.

10. All classes must leave the gym floor by 3 o'clock. Their _____ is necessary so that our teams may practice.

IMPROVING YOUR SPELLING: ADDING SUFFIXES TO WORDS OF MORE THAN ONE SYLLABLE

You will find a world of difference between "An Occurrence at Owl Creek Bridge" and the ordinary short story.

In the above sentence, why is the R in occuR doubled (occuRRence) when -ENCE is added, whereas the R in diffeR is not doubled (diffeRence)?

Here is the explanation:

A. In a word of two or more syllables, we double the final consonant if it is in an **accented** (stressed) syllable before a suffix beginning with a vowel.

WORD	SUFFIXES		NEW WORDS
oc'CUR	+ ed, ing, ence	=	occuRRed, occuRRing, occuRRence
de'FER	+ ed, ing, al	=	defeRRed, defeRRing, defeRRal

B. If the final consonant is in an **unaccented** syllable, do not double the final consonant.

'DIFfer	+ ed, ing, ence	=	diffeRed, diffeRing, diffeRence
proHIB'it	+ ed, ing	=	prohibiTed, prohibiTing

Now that you have learned about occuRRence and diffeRence, you should study the following also:

C. Do not double the final consonant in these cases:

(1) if it comes right after another consonant.

condu $\boxed{c}$ T + ed, ing, or = conducTed, conducTing, conducTor

recomme $\boxed{n}$ D + ed, ing = recommenDed, recommenDing

(2) if it comes right after two vowels.

cont $\boxed{ai}$ N + ed, ing, er = contaiNed, contaiNing, contaiNer

rep $\boxed{ea}$ L + ed, ing = repeaLed, repeaLing

(3) if the accent shifts back to the first syllable.

con'FER + ence = 'CONference
de'FER + ence = 'DEFerence
pre'FER + ence = 'PREFerence
re'FER + ence = 'REFerence

However: ex'CEL + ence = 'EXcellence.

Exercise 11.6: Wordbuilding

I. Write the new word.

	WORD	SUFFIX	NEW WORD
1.	recur	+ ence	= _____
2.	confer	+ ing	= _____
3.	obtain	+ ed	= _____
4.	propel	+ er	= _____
5.	label	+ ed	= _____
6.	regret	+ able	= _____
7.	conceal	+ ing	= _____
8.	occur	+ ed	= _____
9.	prohibit	+ ing	= _____
10.	profit	+ able	= _____
11.	enter	+ ed	= _____
12.	recur	+ ence	= _____
13.	compel	+ ed	= _____
14.	commend	+ able	= _____
15.	permit	+ ed	= _____
16.	excel	+ ence	= _____

17. offer   + ed   = _____

18. appeal   + ing   = _____

19. differ   + ent   = _____

20. recur   + ent   = _____

II. For each word at the left, form the three derivatives indicated.

21. commend   _____ed   _____ing   _____able

22. commit   _____ed   _____ing   _____ment

23. occur   _____ed   _____ing   _____ence

24. prefer   _____ed   _____ing   _____ence

25. regret   _____ed   _____ing   _____able

26. suffer   _____ed   _____ing   _____ance

27. extract   _____ed   _____ing   _____ion

28. open   _____ed   _____ing   _____er

29. defer   _____ed   _____ing   _____ment

30. excel   _____ed   _____ing   _____ence

AVOIDING UNNECESSARY WORDS

A good writer avoids unnecessary words. Ambrose Bierce writes:

"These movements left the condemned man and the sergeant standing on the two ends of the same plank, which spanned three of the cross-ties of the bridge. The end upon which the civilian stood almost, but not quite, reached a fourth." (lines 16–19)

We do not have to ask what the author means by "a fourth." From the previous sentence, we know that he means a *fourth cross-tie*.

In his next sentence, too, the author avoids unnecessary words:

"This plank had been held in place by the weight of the captain; it was now held (he does not repeat *in place*) by that (he does not repeat *the weight*) of the sergeant."

Following the example of Ambrose Bierce, you, too, should remove from your writing any words that repeat an idea already expressed. Note the following:

       QUESTION: Our new gym is the *(finest gym, finest)* in town.
         ANSWER: Our new gym is the *finest* in town.
 EXPLANATION: Since *gym* is mentioned earlier in the sentence, to repeat it
                  is unnecessary.

QUESTION: I didn't hear your answer; please *(repeat it, repeat it again)*.
ANSWER: I didn't hear your answer; please *repeat it*.
EXPLANATION: The word *again* is unnecessary because *repeat* means "say *again.*"

Exercise 11.7: Concise Writing

Rewrite the following sentences, leaving out the unnecessary words.

1. My assignment is completely different from Jane's assignment.

   _____

2. We will wait until we learn the true facts.

   _____

3. The modern kitchen of today uses many appliances.

   _____

4. I have one glove but can't find the other one.

   _____

5. A girl of about eight years old answered the telephone.

   _____

6. The class has finished the first six chapters and is now working on the seventh chapter.

   _____

7. On her head she wore a red and white skating cap.

   _____

8. In my opinion, I believe you are right.

   _____

IMPROVING YOUR COMPOSITION SKILLS: DESCRIBING A PERSON

Reread the first paragraph of the selection on page 141, in which Ambrose Bierce describes the man about to be hanged.

Question: What information does Bierce include in his paragraph?

Answer: In the first four sentences, he offers specific details about the condemned man's

   (a) age (about thirty-five)
   (b) status (a civilian—not an army member)
   (c) occupation (apparently a planter)

(d) dress (wears a well-fitting frock coat)

(e) features (straight nose; firm mouth; broad forehead; long, dark hair; large dark-gray eyes with a kindly expression)

In the final two sentences, Bierce sums up the description with a brief generalization about the man (no vulgar assassin, but apparently a gentleman).

Exercise 11.8: Brief Description of a Person

In a paragraph of about seventy-five words, describe a person. Begin by offering specific details about the person's appearance. End with a brief generalization. Do not mention the person's name.

Hints for Topics:

Describe someone you saw within the last day or two—for example, a member of your family, a neighbor, a friend, a classmate, a teammate, a mail carrier, a salesclerk, a bank teller.

Sample Description

> **As I was about to enter my building, a freckled, red-haired teenager about an inch or two under six feet hurried out, dressed in swim trunks and carrying a beach towel. I recognized him as one of our new neighbors. He waved and gave me a broad smile as he raced by. Obviously, he is not an unfriendly person.**

Now write your description.

_____

_____

_____

_____

_____

_____

_____

_____

_____

Frederick Douglass, an American Slave

by Frederick Douglass

Frederick Douglass, a slave, escaped to the North in 1838, when he was 21, and quickly became a leader in the struggle to abolish slavery. The following passage deals with his boyhood.

I lived in Master Hugh's family about seven years. During this time, I succeeded in learning to read and write. In accomplishing this, I was compelled to resort to various stratagems. I had no regular teacher. My mistress, who had kindly commenced to
5 instruct me, had, in compliance with the advice and direction of her husband, not only ceased to instruct, but had set her face against my being instructed by any one else. It is due, however, to my mistress to say of her, that she did not adopt this course of treatment immediately. She at first lacked the depravity indis-
10 pensable to shutting me up in mental darkness. It was at least necessary for her to have some training in the exercise of irresponsible power, to make her equal to the task of treating me as though I were a brute.

My mistress was, as I have said, a kind and tenderhearted
15 woman; and in the simplicity of her soul she commenced, when I first went to live with her, to treat me as she supposed one human being ought to treat another. In entering upon the duties of a slaveholder, she did not seem to perceive that I sustained to her the relation of a mere chattel, and that for her to treat me as a
20 human being was not only wrong, but dangerously so. Slavery proved as injurious to her as it did to me. When I went there, she was a pious, warm, and tenderhearted woman. There was no sorrow or suffering for which she had not a tear. She had bread for the hungry, clothes for the naked, and comfort for every

mourner that came within her reach. Slavery soon proved its ability to divest her of these heavenly qualities. Under its influence, the tender heart became stone, and the lamblike disposition gave way to one of tigerlike fierceness. The first step in her downward course was in her ceasing to instruct me. She now commenced to practise her husband's precepts. She finally became even more violent in her opposition than her husband himself. She was not satisfied with simply doing as well as he had commanded; she seemed anxious to do better. Nothing seemed to make her more angry than to see me with a newspaper. She seemed to think that here lay the danger. I have had her rush at me with a face made all up of fury, and snatch from me a newspaper, in a manner that fully revealed her apprehension. She was an apt woman; and a little experience soon demonstrated, to her satisfaction, that education and slavery were incompatible with each other.

From this time I was most narrowly watched. If I was in a separate room any considerable length of time, I was sure to be suspected of having a book, and was at once called to give an account of myself. All this, however, was too late. The first step had been taken. Mistress, in teaching me the alphabet, had given me the *inch,* and no precaution could prevent me from taking the *ell.*

The plan which I adopted, and the one by which I was most successful, was that of making friends of all the little white boys whom I met in the street. As many of these as I could, I converted into teachers. With their kindly aid, obtained at different times and in different places, I finally succeeded in learning to read. When I was sent on errands, I always took my book with me, and by going one part of my errand quickly, I found time to get a lesson before my return. I used also to carry bread with me, enough of which was always in the house, and to which I was always welcome; for I was much better off in this regard than many of the poor white children in our neighborhood. This bread I used to bestow upon the hungry little urchins, who, in return, would give me that more valuable bread of knowledge. I am strongly tempted to give the names of two or three of those little boys, as a testimonial of the gratitude and affection I bear them; but prudence forbids;—not that it would injure me, but it might embarrass them; for it is almost an unpardonable offence to teach slaves to read in this Christian country. It is enough to say of the dear little fellows, that they lived on Philpot Street, very near Durgin and Bailey's shipyard. I used to talk this matter of slavery over with them. I would sometimes say to them, I wished I could be as free as they would be when they got to be men. "You will be free as soon as you are twenty-one, *but I am a slave for life!* Have not I as good a right to be free as you have?" These words used to trouble them; they would express for me the liveliest sympathy, and console me with the hope that something would occur by which I might be free.

Line 9. *depravity:* wickedness   Line 30. *precepts:* teachings

Line 18. *sustained:* bore   Line 37. *apt:* quick to learn

Line 19. *chattel:* piece of property   Lines 61–62. *testimonial:* tribute

Line 22. *pious:* religious   Line 62. *prudence:* good judgment

UNDERSTANDING THE SELECTION

Exercise 12.1: Close Reading

In the blank space, write the *letter* of the choice that best completes the statement or answers the question.

1. The narrator was mainly concerned with ____.

   (A) learning to read
   (B) not causing trouble for his little white teachers
   (C) gaining his freedom
   (D) hiding from his master and mistress the fact that he was continuing his education

2. The selection shows that ____.

   (A) no whites had less to eat than slaves
   (B) slavery hurt only the slaves
   (C) children can be more prejudiced than adults
   (D) slavery was evil for the slave and the slaveholder

3. The reader of the selection may conclude that ____.

   (A) the narrator had no kind words for his mistress because she had mistreated him
   (B) slaves and poor white children were not sent to school
   (C) education made a slave a better slave
   (D) a basically fine human being can, under certain conditions, change for the worse

4. The mistress ____.

   (A) had no skill as a teacher
   (B) had no previous experience as a slaveholder
   (C) never treated the narrator as a human being
   (D) disregarded her husband's commands

5. The last three words in the third paragraph, "taking the *ell*," probably refer to ____.

   (A) the letter "L"   (C) stealing
   (B) becoming a reader   (D) learning the alphabet

6. All the following statements about the narrator are true, EXCEPT ____.

   (A) He became proficient in the art of concealment.
   (B) When he ran an errand, he carried his book.
   (C) He used all his little white street friends as instructors.
   (D) He had access to as much bread as he wanted.

7. The narrator's attitude toward the person who taught him the alphabet is best described as a mixture of _____ .

(A) understanding and gratitude
(B) appreciation and resentment
(C) disappointment and sorrow
(D) bitterness and condemnation

8. Of the following, the best title for the selection would be _____ .

(A) Learning to Read   (C) Making Friends
(B) Thirst for Knowledge (D) On Guard

LEARNING NEW WORDS

Line	Word	Meaning	Typical Use
15	**commence** (v.) kə-'men(t)s	begin; start; enter upon	The troops were instructed to *commence* firing and not to stop until further orders.
		(*ant.* **cease, stop, end**)	After two minutes the officer ordered all firing to *cease*.
72	**console** (v.) kən-'sōl	comfort in times of grief; lessen the suffering of; solace	I sent Myra a "get-well" card to *console* her.
50	**convert** (v.) kən-'vərt	change; alter in form; transform	The afternoon sun should *convert* the morning snow into slush.
26	**divest** (v.) dī-'vest	strip (of clothing, ornament, equipment, etc.); force to give up; deprive	The general *divested* the sergeant of his authority when he demoted him to the rank of private.
62	**gratitude** (n.) 'grat-ə-,t(y)üd	state of being *grateful* (thankful) because of a favor received; thankfulness	It is proper to express *gratitude* when someone does you a favor.
		(*ant.* **ingratitude, ungratefulness**)	Despite all the favors I have done for Brad, he refused to let me use his glove. Did you ever hear of such *ingratitude*?
39	**incompatible** (adj.) ,in-kəm-'pat-ə-bəl	incapable of living or acting together; not in harmony; antagonistic	If Erica and Audrey are on the committee, it will never reach an agreement; they are *incompatible*.

		(*ant.* **compatible**)	I am fortunate to have such a *compatible* partner as Jeff; he is easy to get along with.
9– 10	**indispensable** *(adj.)* ˌin-dis-ˈpen(t)-sə-bəl	absolutely necessary; essential	Food is *indispensable;* we cannot live without it.
		(*ant.* **dispensable**)	When going on a hike, you can leave your hair tonic behind; it's *dispensable.*
21	**injurious** *(adj.)* in-ˈjür-ē-əs	causing *injury* (harm); harmful	Smoking is *injurious* to health.
		(*ant.* **beneficial**)	Our gym class met outdoors to enjoy the *beneficial* effects of fresh air and sunshine.
18	**perceive** *(v.)* pər-ˈsēv	become aware of through the senses; observe; see; realize	I *perceived* by the expression on her face that Amy was upset.
3	**stratagem** *(n.)* ˈstrat-ə-jəm	clever scheme for gaining an end; trick; ruse	A bandaged hand is sometimes a *stratagem* for evading work.

APPLYING WHAT YOU HAVE LEARNED

Exercise 12.2: Sentence Completion

Which of the two choices correctly completes the sentence? Write the *letter* of your answer in the space provided.

1. For Jane and her cousin to ____ is impossible; they are incompatible.

   A. agree   B. quarrel

2. Instead of using a stratagem, I ____.

   A. tried to disguise my voice   B. laid all my cards on the table

3. One way to show gratitude is to ____.

   A. write a "thank-you" note   B. accept favors from nobody

4. Fred was ____ by your injurious remark.

   A. delighted   B. hurt

5. The father consoled his daughter when he noticed her ____.

   A. in tears   B. playing with matches

6. There are now _____ in the converted schoolhouse.

    A. 320 students enrolled   B. four families living

7. Do you perceive what I am driving at, or _____?

    A. are you afraid to take a chance   B. shall I explain it once more

8. Audrey is indispensable to our team; we will _____ without her.

    A. lose   B. do just as well

9. The thief was divested _____.

    A. of his loot   B. for robbery

10. Many a tale commences: "_____."

    A. And they lived happily ever after   B. Once upon a time

Exercise 12.3: Definitions

Each expression below defines a word taught on pages 157–158. Enter that word in the space provided.

_____ **1.** lessen the suffering of

_____ **2.** absolutely necessary

_____ **3.** clever scheme for gaining an end

_____ **4.** enter upon

_____ **5.** not in harmony

_____ **6.** force to give up

_____ **7.** causing harm

_____ **8.** become aware of

_____ **9.** alter in form

_____ **10.** state of being thankful for a favor received

Exercise 12.4: Synonyms and Antonyms

Fill the blanks in column A with the required synonyms or antonyms, selecting them from column B.

	Column A	*Column B*
_____	**1.** synonym for *deprive*	convert
_____	**2.** antonym for *ungratefulness*	divest
_____	**3.** synonym for *realize*	gratitude
_____	**4.** antonym for *beneficial*	perceive
_____	**5.** synonym for *transform*	injurious

LEARNING SOME ROOTS AND DERIVATIVES

Each word in bold type is a *root*. The words below it are its *derivatives*.

commence *(v.)*   Were you present when the program *commenced*?

commencement *(n.)*   Were you present at the *commencement* of the program?

console *(v.)*   We tried to *console* the lost child.

consolable *(adj.)*   At first he appeared not to be *consolable*.

consolation *(n.)*   But our kindness and the candy we offered were a *consolation* to him.

convert *(v.)*   Long ago the alchemists tried to *convert* ordinary metals into gold.

convertible *(adj.)*   They believed that ordinary metals were *convertible* into gold.

conversion *(n.)*   They had faith that such a *conversion* was possible.

grateful *(adj.)*   Ralph is *grateful* for the help you gave him in Spanish.

gratefully *(adv.)*   He *gratefully* admits that without your help he would have failed.

gratitude *(n.)*   By the help you have given him, you have earned his *gratitude*.

incompatible *(adj.)*   I had to share a locker with Sam, but we quarreled from the first day; we were *incompatible*.

incompatibly *(adv.)*   The teacher perceived that we were getting along *incompatibly*.

incompatibility *(n.)*   Because of our *incompatibility*, she assigned each of us to a different partner.

indispensable *(adj.)*   A safe water supply is *indispensable*.

indispensably *(adv.)*   We *indispensably* require a safe water supply.

indispensability *(n.)*   No one can deny the *indispensability* of a safe water supply.

injure *(v.)*   A police record can *injure* a person's career.

injurious *(adj.)*   A police record may prove *injurious* to a person's career.

injury *(n.)*   The name of a youthful offender is usually withheld to prevent *injury* to his career.

perceive *(v.)*	Can you *perceive* a difference between the twins?
perceptible *(adj.)*	The difference is hardly *perceptible.*
perceptibly *(adv.)*	One twin is not too *perceptibly* different from the other.
perception *(n.)*	The difference between them is so slight that it escapes *perception.*
stratagem *(n.)*	When a direct attack on Troy failed, the Greeks used a *stratagem* to capture the city.
strategy *(n.)*	Their *strategy* was to offer the unsuspecting Trojans a huge wooden horse secretly filled with armed Greeks.
strategic *(adj.)*	By this *strategic* move, the Greeks were able to defeat the Trojans.
strategically *(adv.)*	The horse was *strategically* designed to get a body of armed Greeks past the walls of Troy.

Exercise 12.5: Roots and Derivatives

Fill each blank below with the root or derivative just listed that best completes the sentence.

1. Some people never get over their grief; others are _____ .

2. Night was almost done, and the first light of the day was gradually becoming

   _____ .

3. Though we lost, it was nevertheless a(n) _____ to me to know that I had hit a home run.

4. An unkind word may _____ a person as severely as a hammer blow.

5. At night a(n) _____ sofa can be transformed to a bed.

6. From the _____ of the trial to its end, not a single seat in the courtroom was vacant.

7. I am _____ to you for keeping me informed about what was happening in class when I was ill.

8. How can you study for your French final while watching football on TV? These are two _____ activities.

9. Ambush is a(n) _____ device by which a small band can surprise a more powerful foe.

10. The employer did not dismiss any of his most highly skilled workers because of their

    _____ to his business.

The N in the negative prefix **IN-**, meaning "not," as in *indecent*, often changes to another letter. For example:

1. Before a word beginning with L, the prefix IN- becomes IL-, as in *illegal*.

2. Before a word beginning with M or P, the prefix IN- becomes IM-, as in *immortal* and *improper*.

3. Before a word beginning with R, the prefix IN- becomes IR-, as in *irregular*.

On the other hand, the N in the negative prefix **UN-** does not change:

$$
\begin{array}{llll}
\text{un} & + & \text{able} & = \text{unable} \\
\text{un} & + & \text{liked} & = \text{unliked} \\
\text{un} & + & \text{married} & = \text{unmarried} \\
\text{un} & + & \text{natural} & = \text{unnatural} \\
\text{un} & + & \text{paid} & = \text{unpaid} \\
\text{un} & + & \text{reliable} & = \text{unreliable}
\end{array}
$$

Exercise 12.6: Wordbuilding With *UN-*
The first entry has been made as a sample.

1. opened   __unopened_____

2. necessary   _____

3. manageable   _____

4. important   _____

5. spoiled   _____

6. pleasant   _____

7. touched   _____

8. noticeable   _____

9. likely   _____

10. educated   _____

Exercise 12.7: Wordbuilding With *IN-*, *IL-*, *IM-*, and *IR-*

Make the word in column II negative by adding the prefix IN, IL, IM, or IR in column I. Then write the new word in column III. (The first five lines have been done for you as examples.)

	I PREFIX		II WORD		III NEW WORD
1.	in	+	complete	=	**incomplete**
2.	il	+	legal	=	**illegal**
3.	im	+	mortal	=	**immortal**
4.	im	+	proper	=	**improper**
5.	ir	+	regular	=	**irregular**
6.	_____	+	possible	=	_____
7.	_____	+	effective	=	_____
8.	_____	+	logical	=	_____
9.	_____	+	responsible	=	_____
10.	_____	+	mature	=	_____
11.	_____	+	convenient	=	_____
12.	_____	+	religious	=	_____
13.	_____	+	modest	=	_____
14.	_____	+	moral	=	_____
15.	_____	+	legible	=	_____
16.	_____	+	resistible	=	_____
17.	_____	+	patient	=	_____
18.	_____	+	sane	=	_____
19.	_____	+	perceptible	=	_____
20.	_____	+	replaceable	=	_____
21.	_____	+	material	=	_____
22.	_____	+	literate	=	_____
23.	_____	+	probable	=	_____
24.	_____	+	reducible	=	_____
25.	_____	+	compatible	=	_____
26.	_____	+	reversible	=	_____
27.	_____	+	legitimate	=	_____
28.	_____	+	movable	=	_____
29.	_____	+	pure	=	_____
30.	_____	+	consistent	=	_____

USING *WHO*, *WHOM*, AND *WHOSE*

1. **WHO** is used as a subject.

     "My mistress, *who* had kindly commenced to instruct me . . ."

      (*who* is the subject of the verb *had commenced*)

     Who is absent?

      (*who* is the subject of the verb *is*)

2. **WHOM** is used:

   (a) as an object of a verb.

     Frederick Douglass made friends of the boys *whom* he met in the street.

      (*whom* is the object of the verb *met*)

     Whom did you see?

      (*whom* is the object of the verb *did see*)

   (b) as an object of a preposition.

     Dan is the student with *whom* I changed places.

      (*whom* is the object of the preposition *with*)

     From *whom* did you get the information?

      (*whom* is the object of the preposition *from*)

3. **WHOSE** indicates ownership.

     The girl *whose* watch you found is my cousin.

      (*whose* indicates ownership of *watch*)

     Whose glove is this?

      (*whose* indicates ownership of *glove*)

   CAUTION: Do not confuse *whose* with the contraction *who's* meaning "who is."
   Who's (Who is) absent?

Exercise 12.8: Using *Who,* *Whom,* *Whose,* **and** *Who's*

The first entry has been made as a sample.

1. Frederick Douglass gave bread to the hungry lads, _____**who**_____ in return gave him the more valuable bread of knowledge.

2. To _____ should we send the check?

3. I could not tell _____ answer was correct.

4. _____ should we ask?

5. _____ on the telephone?

6. This is my sister Sue, _____ is in the ninth grade.

7. _____ turn is it?

8. Do you know by _____ the book was written?

9. At the entrance I met a teacher _____ I had a year ago.

10. _____ was elected?

11. The girl _____ father is driving us to the game says we must be ready at 7:15.

12. There were only three students _____ received marks higher than 90.

13. _____ making his report today?

14. With _____ are you going to the movie?

15. On the bus I met someone _____ you know quite well.

16. Paul is visiting a classmate _____ plays the guitar.

17. Everyone knew for _____ the warning was meant.

18. _____ is she inviting to her party?

19. Those _____ came late had to stand all through the performance.

20. The teacher from _____ I got the highest mark is Mrs. Seiden.

IMPROVING YOUR COMPOSITION SKILLS: EXPLAINING A PLAN FOR SOLVING A PROBLEM

Reread lines 48–60 on page 155, where Frederick Douglass discusses his plan for solving the problem of learning how to read. Note how briefly and simply he has stated the main features of his plan:

1. Making friends of the little white boys he met in the street and using many of them as teachers;
2. Always taking along his book when he was sent on an errand;
3. Doing his errand quickly to leave time for a lesson; and
4. Rewarding his young teachers with gifts of bread.

Exercise 12.9: Explaining a Plan

In a paragraph of about a hundred words, explain a plan you have used, or could use, to solve a problem. Include only the main features of your plan.

Hints: Explain a plan for solving a problem like one of the following:

    being on time
    keeping your belongings from being stolen
    getting additional time to complete a report or assignment
    reducing the fear of making a speech
    keeping from being overcharged

Sample Explanation

> Several times I found when I got home from a shopping errand that I had been overcharged. To prevent this from happening again, I developed a plan. Its features are quite simple. I take along my pocket calculator when I leave for the supermarket. As I place each item into my shopping cart, I enter its price in the calculator, and in this way I can tell how much I have spent before I reach the checkout counter. If there is a discrepancy when I get my sales slip, I can spot it immediately. So far, my plan is working.

Now write your explanation.

_____

_____

_____

_____

_____

_____

_____

_____

_____

_____

_____

_____

_____

_____

Review III.1: Vocabulary and Spelling

Fill in the missing letters of the word at the right of the definition. Then write the complete word in the blank space.

DEFINITION	WORD	COMPLETE WORD
1. violent and uncontrollable anger	_ _ GE	_____
2. second of two	_ _ _ _ _ ER	_____
3. sudden inclination to act	IMP _ _ _ _	_____
4. absolutely necessary	_ _ _ _ _ SPENSABLE	_____
5. as a rule	GENER _ _ _ _	_____
6. choice between two things	_ _ _ _ RNATIVE	_____
7. make a forceful forward movement	LUN _ _	_____
8. fight against	_ _ SIST	_____
9. not in harmony	INCOM _ _ _ IBLE	_____
10. move about slowly and stealthily	_ _ OWL	_____
11. comfort in time of grief	CONS _ _ _	_____
12. long, sharp, pointed tooth	_ _ NG	_____
13. get away from, by skill or cleverness	EV _ _ _	_____
14. thick growth of bushes and shrubs	_ _ USH	_____
15. soft tissue in most bone cavities	MAR _ _ _	_____
16. clever scheme for gaining an end	STRA _ _ _ EM	_____
17. wildly or uncontrollably excited	_ _ _ _ ZIED	_____

18. act of happening again   RE __ __ RRENCE   _____

19. draw away to a different
    subject   __ __ __ TRACT   _____

20. twist and turn this way
    and that   __ __ ITHE   _____

Review III.2: Antonyms

For each italicized word in column A, write the best *antonym* from column B.

	Column A	Column B
_____	1. feeling of *ungratefulness*	insolent
_____	2. *courteous* reply	exclude
_____	3. *beneficial* effects	ignore
_____	4. *heed* traffic signs	commence
_____	5. with *confidence*	yield
_____	6. likely to *resist*	zeal
_____	7. *end* on time	gratitude
_____	8. absence of *apathy*	submission
_____	9. *admit* no one	apprehension
_____	10. total *resistance*	injurious

Review III.3: Synonyms

To each line below, add a word that has the *same meaning* as the first two words on the line. Choose your words from the vocabulary list.

1. transform; change _____

2. beginner; apprentice _____

3. restrain; curb _____

4. earlier; prior _____

5. whine; cry _____

6. outrage; insult _____

7. deprive; strip _____

8. tip; incline _____

9. obviously; evidently _____

10. realize; see _____

Vocabulary List

former	cub
convert	tilt
indignity	whimper
perceive	apparently
check	divest

Review III.4: Spelling

Fill in the missing letter of the incomplete word in column A. Then write the complete word in column B.

Column A   Column B

1. occurr __ nce   _____

2. min __ te   _____

3. confid __ nt   _____

4. i __ convenient   _____

5. resist __ nce   _____

6. gramm __ r   _____

7. assist __ nt   _____

8. i __ logical   _____

9. appli __ nce   _____

10. sep __ rate   _____

11. vehem __ nt   _____

12. w __ men   _____

13. ignor __ nt   _____

14. i __ patient   _____

15. allegi __ nce   _____

16. sug __ r   _____

17. interfer __ nce   _____

18. i __ responsible   _____

19. observ __ nt   _____

20. i __ moral   _____

Review III.5: Wordbuilding

Write the new word.

WORD + SUFFIX = NEW WORD

1. compel + ed   = _____

2. offer + ing   = _____

3. repeal + ed   = _____

4. commit + ment = _____

5. label + ed   = _____

6. refer + ing = _____

7. benefit + ing = _____

8. regret + able = _____

9. permit + ing = _____

10. prefer + ence = _____

Review III.6: Sentence Completion

Complete each sentence below with the most appropriate word from the following vocabulary list.

Vocabulary List

former	incompatible	lunge
gratitude	latter	frantic
indignity	alternative	indispensable
convert	writhe	check

1. Near dismissal time, some students are so impatient that they _____ in their seats.

2. I hope Laura and I will not be assigned to the same committee because we are _____ .

3. The opposing team tried to _____ our advance at the twenty-yard line, but we swept on to a touchdown.

4. To bite the hand that feeds you is no way to show _____ .

5. If you decide neither to resist nor to surrender, you will still have a third _____ : to try to arrange a truce.

6. Both silver and gold are precious metals, but the _____ is more costly.

7. When you cross the border, you will have to _____ some of your money to Canadian currency.

8. The _____ screams of a lost child distracted our attention.

9. If Joan quits, we can still put on the play; she's not _____ .

10. To be called lazy is an insult, but to be labeled as a liar is a far greater _____ .

Review III.7: Roots and Derivatives

On lines B and C, write the required forms of the italicized word on line A.

1. A. Are you *resistant* to change?

   B. Do you _____ change because you prefer things to remain as they are?

   C. Do you go along with new ideas, or do you offer _____?

2. A. I have an *impulse* to swing at the first pitch.

   B. I _____ swing at the first pitch.

   C. I am _____ about swinging at the first pitch.

3. A. Some members of the squad refuse to *submit* to your authority.

   B. They will not _____ obey your orders.

   C. They will not be _____.

4. A. Certain plant diseases, if *unchecked,* can destroy entire crops.

   B. Farmers spray crops to _____ plant disease.

   C. They have successfully used sprays as a _____ to crop destruction.

5. A. Before the interview, I was *apprehensive.*

   B. I came to the interview with _____.

   C. I entered the interviewer's office _____.

6. A. Arthur and Alex cannot work as a team because they are *incompatible.*

   B. They are _____ matched and should be separated.

   C. Because of their _____, they are unlikely to produce any useful work.

7. A. Why were you *insolent* to your cousin?

   B. Why did you _____ slam the door in his face?

   C. There is no reason for such _____.

8. A. The *prowler* sighted near the farm could have been a fox or a wolf.

   B. At night these beasts _____ in search of food.

   C. A fox might have been on the _____ on the outskirts of the farm.

9. A. The picnic is *exclusively* for members who have paid their dues.

   B. We plan to _____ all others.

   C. The threat of _____ from the picnic has already made several members pay up.

10. A. Harvey's cough is apt to *recur* when he is run down.

    B. He has a _____ cough.

    C. It seems to get worse with each _____.

11. A. It is possible to *convert* some waste material into useful products.

 B. Some waste materials are _____ to useful products.

 C. One example is the _____ of dead leaves into compost for fertilizing the soil.

12. A. False rumors may *injure* a person's reputation.

 B. False rumors may do serious _____ to a person's reputation.

 C. False rumors may be _____ .

13. A. My opponent *evaded* me.

 B. My opponent was _____ .

 C. My opponent _____ stepped to one side.

14. A. You ought to call on Marie to *console* her.

 B. She does not seem _____ , but I know you can cheer her up.

 C. I am sure she will find _____ in your words of sympathy.

15. A. We are *grateful* for your help.

 B. We _____ appreciate what you have done for us.

 C. We wish to express our _____ .

16. A. The commander's *strategy* was to retreat to a more favorable position.

 B. He ordered a retreat for _____ reasons.

 C. He perceived that, under the circumstances, retreat was _____ necessary.

17. A. No one has shown greater *zeal* in selling tickets than Barbara.

 B. No one has been more _____ than she.

 C. Barbara is working _____ to sell more tickets.

18. A. The fog made it difficult to *perceive* what lay ahead.

 B. Nearby objects were barely _____ .

 C. The fog made _____ difficult.

19. A. It would be very difficult for a library to be without dictionaries and encyclopedias; such reference books are *indispensable*.

 B. Reference books are _____ needed.

 C. Because of their _____ , reference books are among the first that a library should purchase.

20. A. On long trips, Dad and Mom *alternate* behind the wheel.

 B. Before starting out, Dad usually gives Mom the _____ of driving.

 C. They change places every hour so that each of them is _____ the driver or a passenger.

Review III.8: Concise Writing

Rewrite the following 160-word incident in the space provided, keeping all its ideas but reducing the number of words. Try to use no more than 112 words.

> As a rule, every member who asks for the floor is given a chance to speak. However, our president does not get along well with our newest member. At the last meeting that we had, he refused to take notice of this member, though the latter had had his hand up for a considerable period of time.
>
> "You can't do this!" shouted the member. "It is your duty to recognize me! Don't avoid facing up to that duty! The club is discussing something! You can't bar me from participation!"
>
> The president, who is good at clever schemes for gaining his ends, tried to draw our attention to an entirely different subject. The member took this as another offense to his sense of personal dignity and self-respect. He flew into a fit of violent, uncontrollable anger. When we saw him make a sudden forceful movement in the direction of the president, several of us stepped in to prevent a fight.

The Redheaded League

by Sir Arthur Conan Doyle

Sherlock Holmes, the famous detective, has been listening to Mr. Jabez Wilson, who has come for help. In walks Dr. Watson, Holmes's close friend and assistant. Holmes proceeds to inform Watson about the Wilson case.

"Now, Mr. Jabez Wilson here has been good enough to call upon me this morning, and to begin a narrative which promises to be one of the most singular which I have listened to for some time. You have heard me remark that the strangest and most
5 unique things are very often connected not with the larger but with the smaller crimes, and occasionally, indeed, where there is room for doubt whether any positive crime has been committed. As far as I have heard, it is impossible for me to say whether the present case is an instance of crime or not, but the course of events
10 is certainly among the most singular that I have ever listened to. Perhaps, Mr. Wilson, you would have the great kindness to recommence your narrative. I ask you not merely because my friend Dr. Watson has not heard the opening part but also because the peculiar nature of the story makes me anxious to have every
15 possible detail from your lips. As a rule, when I have heard some slight indication of the course of events, I am able to guide myself by the thousands of other similar cases which occur to my memory. In the present instance I am forced to admit that the facts are, to the best of my belief, unique."

20 The portly client puffed out his chest with an appearance of some little pride and pulled a dirty and wrinkled newspaper from the inside pocket of his great-coat. As he glanced down the advertisement column, with his head thrust forward and the paper flat-

tened out upon his knee, I took a good look at the man and endea-
vored, after the fashion of my companion, to read the indications
which might be presented by his dress or appearance.

I did not gain very much, however, by my inspection. Our visitor bore every mark of being an average commonplace British
tradesman, obese, pompous, and slow. He wore rather baggy gray
shepherd's check trousers, a not overclean black frock coat, unbuttoned in the front, and a drab waistcoat with a heavy brassy Albert
chain, and a square pierced bit of metal dangling down as an ornament. A frayed top hat and a faded brown overcoat with a wrinkled velvet collar lay upon a chair beside him. Altogether, look as
I would, there was nothing remarkable about the man save his
blazing red head, and the expression of extreme chagrin and discontent upon his features.

Sherlock Holmes's quick eye took in my occupation, and he
shook his head with a smile as he noticed my questioning glances.
"Beyond the obvious facts that he has at some time done manual
labor, that he takes snuff, that he is a Freemason, that he has
been in China, and that he has done a considerable amount of
writing lately, I can deduce nothing else."

Mr. Jabez Wilson started up in his chair, with his forefinger
upon the paper, but his eyes upon my companion.

"How, in the name of good fortune, did you know all that, Mr.
Holmes?" he asked. "How did you know, for example, that I did
manual labor? It's as true as gospel, for I began as a ship's
carpenter."

"Your hands, my dear sir. Your right hand is quite a size larger
than your left. You have worked with it, and the muscles are more
developed."

Line 36. *chagrin:* disappointment

Line 41. *Freemason:* member of a worldwide, secret society

UNDERSTANDING THE SELECTION

Exercise 13.1: Close Reading

In the blank space, write the *letter* of the choice that best completes the statement or
answers the question.

1. In the opening paragraph, Holmes _____.

    (A) addresses first Dr. Watson and then Mr. Wilson
    (B) addresses Dr. Watson but not Mr. Wilson
    (C) is forced to admit that he cannot help Mr. Wilson
    (D) addresses first Mr. Wilson and then Dr. Watson

2. In the second paragraph, "I" refers to ____.

(A) Holmes, and "companion" to Mr. Wilson
(B) Holmes, and "companion" to Dr. Watson
(C) Dr. Watson, and "companion" to Holmes
(D) Dr. Watson, and "companion" to Mr. Wilson

3. The selection suggests that ____.

(A) Mr. Wilson is a well-to-do merchant
(B) a newspaper advertisement has something to do with the case
(C) Dr. Watson is not interested in the case
(D) some of Holmes's statements about Mr. Wilson's past may not be true

4. The fact that Mr. Wilson is ____ escapes Dr. Watson's attention.

(A) right-handed
(B) redheaded
(C) slow
(D) not neatly dressed

5. The selection indicates that ____.

(A) Holmes has not the slightest doubt about his ability to solve the case
(B) Wilson has finished telling his story
(C) Holmes is certain that a crime has been committed
(D) Dr. Watson has not said anything to Holmes or to the visitor

6. Dr. Watson is all of the following EXCEPT ____.

(A) a friend of Holmes
(B) a police official
(C) a companion of Holmes
(D) the narrator of the story

7. The things about Mr. Wilson that Holmes notices are ____ than those that Dr. Watson notices.

(A) less astonishing
(B) more obvious
(C) less important
(D) less obvious

8. Which of the following statements about Mr. Wilson are TRUE? ____

    I.   He does not listen attentively.
    II. He hesitates in his speech.
    III. He is immaculate.
    IV. He uses poor English.

(A) I and III only
(B) IV only
(C) II and IV only
(D) None

Line	Word	Meaning	Typical Use
20	**client** *(n.)* 'klī-ənt	person who engages the professional services of another; customer; patron	If you need insurance, get in touch with Watts and Miller. My uncle has been one of their *clients* for years.
28	**commonplace** *(adj.)* 'käm-ən-ˌplās	ordinary; unremarkable; neither new nor interesting (*ant.* **extraordinary**)	The plot is *commonplace,* like that of most Westerns, but the acting is *extraordinary.*
43	**deduce** *(v.)* di-'d(y)üs	reason out or conclude from known facts; infer	From the fact that an ambulance was in their driveway, I *deduced* that someone in their family was ill.
33	**frayed** *(adj.)* 'frād	worn; ragged; worn out	I have given that sweater a great deal of wear; it is getting *frayed* at the cuffs.
40	**manual** *(adj.)* 'man-yə(-wə)l	1. involving the hands	A good typist has a high degree of *manual* skill.
		2. hand-operated	In cars with *manual* transmission, the driver shifts gears by hand.
		3. requiring or using physical skill or energy	Because he likes working with his hands, Frank will go into carpentry or some other kind of *manual* occupation.
12	**narrative** *(n.)* 'nar-ət-iv	something that is *narrated* (told); story; tale; account	After dinner, we listened to my cousin's *narrative* of his camping trip.
32–33	**ornament** *(n.)* 'ȯr-nə-mənt	something that adorns or adds beauty; decoration; embellishment	With a plain dress, Grandma wears a jeweled pin, a necklace, or some other simple *ornament.*
29	**pompous** *(adj.)* 'päm-pəs	making an appearance of importance or dignity; self-important	Sheila did not wear her medal because she felt it would make her seem *pompous.*

| | | (*ant.* **lowly**) | Andrew Carnegie rose from a *lowly* position in a cotton mill to become one of the most important leaders of American industry. |

| 20 | **portly** (*adj.*)
 'pōrt-lē | heavy of body; stout; corpulent; obese | Regent Tailors can outfit individuals of all sizes, whether short or tall, lean or *portly*. |
| | | (*ant.* **lean, skinny**) | |

| 19 | **unique** (*adj.*)
 yü-'nēk | being the only one of its kind in existence; having no like or equal; unparalleled; singular | Do you realize that everyone is a *unique* individual, since no two persons are exactly alike? |
| | | (*ant.* **common, ordinary**) | Don't think your mistake is unique. Others have made it, too. In fact, it is quite *common*. |

APPLYING WHAT YOU HAVE LEARNED

Exercise 13.2: Sentence Completion

Which of the two choices correctly completes the sentence? Write the *letter* of your answer in the space provided.

1. Her drawings are commonplace; there is nothing ____ about them.

   A. remarkable   B. ordinary

2. One of the teams has the pompous name of ____ .

   A. "Grand Monarchs"   B. "Blue Jays"

3. To ____ is a unique achievement.

   A. be elected President of the United States   B. break the world's record in the high jump

4. You cannot deduce anything unless you start ____ .

   A. with facts   B. without delay

5. The ____ and his client were here a moment ago.

   A. lawyer   B. customer

6. She wore a ____ as an ornament.

   A. puzzled look   B. bracelet

7. _____ requires manual skill

    A. Listening to an opera   B. Rowing a boat

8. Uncle Jim has become portly; he has _____ much weight.

    A. lost   B. gained

9. It was a narrative that I had not _____ before.

    A. heard   B. eaten

10. Some trousers become frayed; others _____.

    A. are hard to clean   B. wear like iron

Exercise 13.3: Definitions

Each expression below defines a word taught on pages 177–178. Enter that word in the space provided.

_____ **1.** involving the hands

_____ **2.** neither new nor interesting

_____ **3.** having no like or equal

_____ **4.** something that is told

_____ **5.** something that adorns

_____ **6.** reason out from known facts

_____ **7.** heavy of body

_____ **8.** person who engages the professional services of another

_____ **9.** worn out

_____ **10.** making an appearance of importance

Exercise 13.4: Synonyms and Antonyms

A. Replace the italicized word or expression with a _synonym_ from the vocabulary list on the next page.

_____ **1.** The Puritans wore very plain clothing, without _decoration_ or embellishment.

_____ **2.** English bicycles are equipped with _hand_ brakes.

_____ **3.** The accountant was about to leave the office when a _customer_ called.

_____ **4.** Have you read "An Occurrence at Owl Creek Bridge"? It is a most unusual _tale_.

_____ **5.** He will not wear a shirt with a *ragged* collar.

_____ **6.** What have you been able to *infer* from the facts I have given you?

B. Replace each italicized word with an *antonym* from the vocabulary list.

_____ **7.** The table seemed to be a *common* piece of furniture.

_____ **8.** The person we talked to impressed us as being a *lowly* individual.

_____ **9.** The room was decorated with *extraordinary* furnishings.

_____ **10.** At the next station, a *lean,* middle-aged woman got off the train.

Vocabulary List

deduce	commonplace
narrative	manual
portly	pompous
frayed	ornament
unique	client

LEARNING SOME ROOTS AND DERIVATIVES

Each word in bold type is a *root*. The words below it are its *derivatives.*

deduce *(v.)*	From the few clues we have so far, we can *deduce* very little.
deducible *(adj.)*	This much is *deducible:* the thief, whoever he is, was careful not to leave many clues behind.
deduction *(n.)*	About the only *deduction* we can make at this time is that the thief is a shrewd operator.
manual *(adj.)*	In the olden days, pumping water from a well was a *manual* operation.
manually *(adv.)*	Today, water does not have to be pumped *manually*—we have electric pumps.
narrate *(v.)*	Have you heard my cousin Joan *narrate* the details of her trip to Alaska?
narrative *(n.)*	It's an exciting *narrative.*
narrator *(n.)*	Joan is an excellent *narrator.*
narration *(n.)*	She excels in *narration.*

ornament *(n.)*	Buttons and bows can be useful as *ornaments*.
ornament *(v.)*	For example, buttons of various colors, shapes, and sizes, are used to *ornament* garments.
ornamental *(adj.)*	Bows are prized for their *ornamental* value in gift-wrapping.
ornamentation *(n.)*	Buttons and bows are widely used in *ornamentation*.
pomp *(n.)*	The old emperor enjoyed the *pomp* and splendor of reviewing his troops as their commander in chief.
pompous *(adj.)*	A *pompous* man, he loved to appear in public in dress uniform.
pompously *(adv.)*	His uniforms were *pompously* ornamented with rows of medals and ribbons.
pomposity *(n.)*	The emperor's daughter, however, disapproved of such *pomposity;* she disliked parades, titles, and uniforms.
portly *(adj.)*	One clown was tall and lean; the other was short and *portly*.
portliness *(n.)*	Because of his *portliness,* the short clown could not run too fast.
unique *(adj.)*	Gibraltar is in a *unique* position near the entrance to the Mediterranean Sea.
uniquely *(adv.)*	Gibraltar is *uniquely* situated.
uniqueness *(n.)*	Gibraltar has been highly prized as a naval base because of the *uniqueness* of its location.

Exercise 13.5: Roots and Derivatives

Fill each blank below with the root or derivative just listed that best completes the sentence.

1. Gordon often spoils a story in telling it; he is not a good _____ .

2. The new office manager _____ insisted that all of the clerks address him as "Sir."

3. When I saw your books were still on your desk, I made the _____ that you had not yet left for home.

4. The _____ of St. Augustine, Florida, is that it is the oldest city in the United States, having been founded in 1565.

5. From the restaurant owner's _____ , you might deduce that he likes to eat.

6. As a little child, I loved to hear my mother _____ fairy tales.

7. This has been a(an) _____ wet year; we have had more rain than in any previous year on record.

8. Before the invention of the electric can opener, all can openers were operated

_____.

9. When Eva is not playing her handsome guitar, she uses it to _____ the wall of her room.

10. Unfortunately the owner's name was not _____ from the contents of the purse.

IMPROVING YOUR SPELLING: DROPPING PREFIXES AND SUFFIXES

It is often possible to change derivatives into root words by dropping prefixes and suffixes.

discontent − DIS = content
developed − ED = develop
unbuttoned − UN. . .ED = button

CAUTIONS:

1. If an E was dropped when the suffix was added, put back the E.

blaze + ING = blazing
blazing − ING = blaze

2. If a final consonant was doubled when the suffix was added, undouble it.

commit + ED = committed
committed − ED = commit

bag + y = baggy
baggy − y = bag

3. If a final Y was changed to I when the suffix was added, change it back to Y.

hurry + ED = hurried
hurried − ED = hurry

happy + NESS = happiness
happiness − NESS = happy

Exercise 13.6: Changing Derivatives to Roots
Write the root word in the column at the right.

1. remarkable   − able   = _____

2. dangling   − ing   = _____

3. bigger   – er   = _____

4. disappearance   – dis *and* ance   = _____

5. foggy   – y   = _____

6. unopened   – un *and* ed   = _____

7. pompous   – ous   = _____

8. planning   – ing   = _____

9. unhappiness   – un *and* ness   = _____

10. permitted   – ed   = _____

11. advertisement   – ment   = _____

12. brassy   – y   = _____

13. unreliable   – un *and* able   = _____

14. improperly   – im *and* ly   = _____

15. listener   – er   = _____

16. flattened   – en *and* ed   = _____

17. frayed   – ed   = _____

18. hottest   – est   = _____

19. indescribable   – in *and* able   = _____

20. recommence   – re   = _____

21. visitor   – or   = _____

22. inescapable   – in *and* able   = _____

23. compelled   – ed   = _____

24. weariness   – ness   = _____

25. wrinkled   – ed   = _____

USING ACTIVE AND PASSIVE VERBS

1. An **active verb** describes an action done by its subject.

   Sherlock Holmes <u>solved</u> the case.
           v

   (The verb *solved* is active because it describes an action done by *Sherlock Holmes*, its subject.)

2. A **passive verb** describes an action done to its subject.

   The case <u>was solved</u> by Sherlock Holmes.
         v

   (The verb *was solved* is passive because it describes an action done to the *case*, its subject.)

Reading Selection 13: The Redheaded League   **183**

Here are some further examples of active and passive verbs:

ACTIVE: Carelessness *causes* accidents.
PASSIVE: Accidents *are caused* by carelessness.

ACTIVE: She *will write* the letter.
PASSIVE: The letter *will be written* by her.

ACTIVE: The children *ate* the chocolates.
PASSIVE: The chocolates *were eaten* by the children.

3. You can form the passive by adding some form of the verb *to be* (*is, was, will be, has been*, etc.) to the past participle (third principal part) of a verb. Examples:

is broken   *has been collected*   *was introduced*
will be told   *are being sent*   *were misplaced*

Exercise 13.7:   Changing Active Verbs to Passive Verbs

SAMPLE: The Giants won the game.
The game was won by the Giants.

1. A passerby noticed the fire.

_____

2. Exercise develops muscles.

_____

3. Mr. Wilson did manual labor.

_____

4. Dad will pay the bill.

_____

5. The courts enforce the laws.

_____

4. In general, use *active* verbs. They will enable you to express yourself more clearly, more briefly, and more naturally.

Compare these sentences:

PASSIVE: The car was washed by us.   (6 words)
ACTIVE: We washed the car.   (4 words)

Not only does the second sentence use fewer words, but it is clearer and more natural. The use of the passive verb in the first sentence makes that sentence unnatural and awkward.

Active verbs are far more common in English than are passive verbs. Avoid passive verbs, especially when they cause awkwardness.

5. One good use of passive verbs is to help you avoid the vague pronoun *they,* as in the following:

POOR: *They* manufacture automobiles in Detroit.

(Who is *they?* The sentence is not clear on this point. Probably *they* is a vague reference to the automobile factories, or the automobile manufacturers.)

In a case like the above, use a passive verb to avoid vagueness:

BETTER: Automobiles *are manufactured* in Detroit.

Exercise 13.8: Using Active and Passive Verbs to Improve Writing

Improve each of the following sentences by rewriting it with an active or a passive verb, as needed.

SAMPLES: An agreement will be entered into by us.
We will enter into an agreement.

They sell refreshments in the lobby.
Refreshments are sold in the lobby.

1. Six kittens were had by our cat.

_____

2. A good look at Mr. Wilson was taken by Dr. Watson.

_____

3. Your help is urgently needed by me.

_____

4. They grow excellent corn in Iowa.

_____

5. A good time will be had by you.

_____

6. Their new uniforms were received by the players.

_____

7. Baggy pants were worn by Mr. Wilson.

_____

8. They arrest reckless drivers in this town.

_____

9. Our seats will be taken promptly by us.

_____

10. The moon was jumped over by the cow.

_____

IMPROVING YOUR COMPOSITION SKILLS: ACHIEVING UNITY

A paragraph has *unity* if it deals with one main topic and all its sentences stick to that topic.

For a good example of unity, reread the paragraph from *The Redheaded League* in which Dr. Watson tells what he gained from his observation of Mr. Jabez Wilson (page 175, lines 27–37). Note the characteristics of that paragraph:

1. The first sentence states the topic: *I did not gain very much, however, by my inspection.*

2. All the other sentences stick to that topic. They show that Dr. Watson saw only the more obvious details about Mr. Jabez Wilson and therefore failed to make any startling discoveries.

Question: Which sentences, if any, spoil the unity of the following paragraph?

> **Pam has an excellent record of school service. She has regularly served as an usher at school plays and as a receptionist on open-school nights. Since her sophomore year, she has played the piano in the school orchestra. As class president, she has provided leadership in improving relations between the school and the senior citizens of the community. In addition, she is an outstanding scholar. Her name has always been on the honor roll.**

Answer: The last two sentences are off the topic—they have nothing to do with Pam's service to the school. They should be removed from the paragraph.

Exercise 13.9: Writing a Unified Paragraph

Develop one of the following topic sentences—or one of your own—into a unified paragraph. Your paragraph should have no more than five or six sentences, but make sure that every one of them is on the topic.

Hints for Topic Sentences:

1. Many commercials are downright boring.
2. Electricity is indispensable in our daily living.
3. _____ is a friend I can depend on.
4. I am in favor of (or opposed to) junk mail.
5. Some penalties are too harsh (or too lenient).

Below, write your unified paragraph.

_____

_____

_____

_____

_____

_____

_____

_____

_____

White Fang

by Jack London

It is fifty below zero. Down a frozen waterway, a team of dogs is dragging a sled with a coffin lashed to it. Ahead of the dogs, a man in snowshoes is plodding his way through the snow, and behind the sled is a second man. A third man has died; his corpse is in the coffin.

An hour went by, and a second hour. The pale light of the short sunless day was beginning to fade, when a faint far cry arose on the still air. It soared upward with a swift rush, till it reached its topmost note, where it persisted, palpitant and tense, and then
5 slowly died away. It might have been a lost soul wailing, had it not been invested with a certain sad fierceness and hungry eagerness. The front man turned his head until his eyes met the eyes of the man behind. And then, across the narrow oblong box, each nodded to the other.
10 A second cry arose, piercing the silence with needlelike shrillness. Both men located the sound. It was to the rear, somewhere in the snowy expanse they had just traversed. A third and answering cry arose, also to the rear and to the left of the second cry.
15 "They're after us, Bill," said the man at the front.

His voice sounded hoarse and unreal, and he had spoken with apparent effort.

"Meat is scarce," answered his comrade. "I ain't seen a rabbit sign for days."
20 Thereafter they spoke no more, though their ears were keen for the hunting-cries that continued to rise behind them.

At the fall of darkness they swung the dogs into a cluster of spruce trees on the edge of the waterway and made a camp. The

coffin, at the side of the fire, served for seat and table. The wolf-
25   dogs, clustered on the far side of the fire, snarled and bickered
among themselves, but evinced no inclination to stray off into the
darkness.

"Seems to me, Henry, they're stayin' remarkable close to
camp," Bill commented.

30   Henry, squatting over the fire and settling the pot of coffee
with a piece of ice, nodded. Nor did he speak till he had taken his
seat on the coffin and begun to eat.

"They know where their hides is safe," he said. "They'd sooner
eat grub than be grub. They're pretty wise, them dogs."

35   Bill shook his head. "Oh, I don't know."

His comrade looked at him curiously. "First time I ever heard
you say anythin' about their not bein' wise."

"Henry," said the other, munching with deliberation the beans
he was eating, "did you happen to notice the way them dogs kicked
40   up when I was a-feedin' 'em?"

"They did cut up more'n usual," Henry acknowledged.

"How many dogs 've we got, Henry?"

"Six."

"Well, Henry . . ." Bill stopped for a moment, in order that his
45   words might gain greater significance. "As I was sayin', Henry,
we've got six dogs. I took six fish out of the bag. I gave one fish to
each dog, an', Henry, I was one fish short."

"You counted wrong."

"We've got six dogs," the other reiterated dispassionately. "I
50   took out six fish. One Ear didn't get no fish. I come back to the
bag afterward an' got 'im his fish."

"We've only got six dogs," Henry said.

"Henry," Bill went on, "I won't say they was all dogs, but there
was seven of 'em that got fish."

UNDERSTANDING THE SELECTION

Exercise 14.1: Close Reading

In the blank space, write the *letter* of the choice that best completes the statement or
answers the question.

1. Bill suggests that _____.

(A) he made a mistake in counting
(B) one of the dogs got two fish
(C) his imagination played a trick on him
(D) one of the animals that got fish was not a dog

2. Which of the following is UNTRUE? ____

(A) The sun shone only a short time each day.
(B) The men and dogs did not travel at night.
(C) The men did not see who was making the cries.
(D) One Ear is the name of a dog.

3. The dogs ____.

(A) made answering cries
(B) did not like fish
(C) were part wolf
(D) were fed by Henry

4. The cries ____.

(A) came from a single source
(B) were made by hungry creatures
(C) could be heard on all sides of the traveling party
(D) were only three in number

5. According to the evidence in the selection, ____.

(A) the dogs feel unsafe, but not the men
(B) both the men and the dogs feel safe
(C) both the men and the dogs feel unsafe
(D) the men feel unsafe, but not the dogs

6. There is evidence that ____.

(A) Bill is the front man
(B) the dogs are fed after the men have eaten
(C) Henry is less aware than Bill about what has already happened
(D) the men have beans, fish, and coffee for dinner

7. All the following statements are true, EXCEPT ____.

(A) Henry is the first to speak.
(B) "Grub" (line 34) means "food."
(C) The men communicate with each other by words only.
(D) "Kicked up" (lines 39–40) means the same as "cut up" (line 41).

8. Which of the following correctly describe the conversation? ____

    I. It is not perfectly grammatical.
    II. It is concise.
    III. It consists of statements and questions.
    IV. There is considerable variation in sentence length.

(A) I, II, and III only
(B) I and III only
(C) I and IV only
(D) I, II, III, and IV

Line	Word	Meaning	Typical Use
41	**acknowledge** (v.) ak-'näl-ij	admit to be true; admit; concede (*ant.* **deny**)	At first Cindy denied that she was the owner of the water pistol, but she finally *acknowledged* that it was hers.
25	**bicker** (v.) 'bik-ər	quarrel over petty things; wrangle; squabble	Almost every day, I would hear the brothers quarrel, and I often wondered what they were *bickering* about.
22	**cluster** (n.) kləs-tər	number of similar things growing or grouped together; bunch	We bought a *cluster* of red grapes that weighed more than two pounds.
49	**dispassionately** (adv.) dis-'pash-(ə-)nət-lē	in a *dispassionate* (calm) manner; calmly; coolly (*ant.* **passionately**)	The first defendant listened *dispassionately* to the verdict; he showed no emotion at all. But the second shouted *passionately:* "It's a frame-up! I am innocent!"
26	**evince** (v.) i-'vin(t)s	display clearly; show; reveal	The parents were alarmed, but in the children's presence they *evinced* no sign of fright.
2	**fade** (v.) 'fād	grow dim; lose brightness or color; disappear gradually; wither	It was getting late. Daylight was *fading*. Soon it would be dark.
4	**persist** (v.) pər-'sist	1. go on resolutely despite opposition, warnings, or pleas; persevere (*ant.* **desist**) 2. last on and on; continue to exist	Why do you *persist* in calling me Deborah? Please call me Debbie. The government order directed the company to *desist* from making false claims. The cold medicines have not helped; my cough has *persisted*.
45	**significance** (n.) sig-'nif-i-kən(t)s	quality of being *significant* (important); importance; consequence; meaning	Today's brief quiz was not too important. The final will be of far greater *significance*.

(*ant.* **insignificance**)

Wanda insists on paying back the dime she borrowed, but I told her to forget about that debt because of its *insignificance.*

3	**soar** (*v.*)	fly upward; move upward; rise; ascend	Stock prices *soared* in the morning but fell sharply by midafternoon.
	′sō(ə)r		
12	**traverse** (*v.*)	pass through or over; cross	Thousands of pioneer families *traversed* the Great Plains in covered wagons.
	trə-′vərs		

APPLYING WHAT YOU HAVE LEARNED

Exercise 14.2: Sentence Completion

Which of the two choices correctly completes the sentence? Write the *letter* of your answer in the space provided.

1. Will the pain _____ or persist?

    A. continue   B. stop

2. She talked dispassionately, as if she were _____.

    A. not the least bit concerned   B. out for revenge

3. The _____ soared.

    A. kite   B. lion

4. In his campaign speeches, Henry evinced _____.

    A. his opponents   B. a sense of humor

5. Ruth _____, but she will not acknowledge it.

    A. admits her mistake   B. knows she is wrong

6. We traversed the playing field _____.

    A. on foot   B. without leaving our seats

7. There is no reason for them to bicker, since they _____.

    A. both agree   B. do not trust each other

8. You said these details are _____, but I find them of no significance.

    A. meaningless   B. important

9. As dawn approaches, the stars fade and _____.

    A. disappear   B. grow bright

10. When I entered the gym, I saw a cluster of my friends, and I wondered why they were all _____.

    A. avoiding one another   B. together

Exercise 14.3: Definitions

Each expression below defines a word taught on pages 191–192. Enter that word in the space provided.

_____ **1.** move upward

_____ **2.** display clearly

_____ **3.** number of similar things grouped together

_____ **4.** grow dim

_____ **5.** pass through or over

_____ **6.** admit to be true

_____ **7.** quality of being important

_____ **8.** quarrel over petty things

_____ **9.** in a calm manner

_____ **10.** go on resolutely despite opposition

Exercise 14.4: Synonyms and Antonyms

Fill the blanks in column A with the required synonyms or antonyms, selecting them from column B.

	Column A	Column B
_____	**1.** synonym for *bunch*	insignificance
_____	**2.** antonym for *importance*	desist
_____	**3.** synonym for *cross*	passionately
_____	**4.** synonym for *rise*	acknowledge
_____	**5.** antonym for *deny*	evince
_____	**6.** antonym for *calmly*	traverse
_____	**7.** synonym for *wrangle*	cluster
_____	**8.** synonym for *show*	fade
_____	**9.** antonym for *persevere*	soar
_____	**10.** synonym for *wither*	bicker

LEARNING SOME ROOTS AND DERIVATIVES

Each word in bold type is a *root*. The words below it are its *derivatives*.

acknowledge *(v.)*   To hoist a white flag is to ask for a truce or *acknowledge* defeat.

acknowledgment *(n.)*   The raising of a white flag can be an *acknowledgment* of surrender.

bicker *(v.)*   The difference between your price and my offer is trifling; let's not *bicker* about it.

bickering *(n.)*   All right. I'll give you another dollar, if that will stop the *bickering.*

cluster *(n.)*   By 9 A.M. a *cluster* of people had gathered on the steps of the library, waiting for the doors to open.

cluster *(v.)*   Before leaving, all of us *clustered* around Harvey to wish him once more a happy birthday.

dispassionate *(adj.)*   If my sister were involved in a fight, I could not be a *dispassionate* onlooker.

dispassionately *(adv.)*   If I were to see my sister being hurt, I could not stand by *dispassionately.*

persist *(v.)*   The convict *persisted* in his efforts to get a new trial.

persistent *(adj.)*   He was *persistent;* he wrote hundreds of letters to public officials.

persistently *(adv.)*   Several lawyers told him there was no hope, but he *persistently* continued his campaign.

persistence *(n.)*   His *persistence* was finally rewarded when a higher court ordered that he be given a retrial.

significant *(adj.)*   At the first trial, the convict's attorneys had not introduced a certain piece of evidence because they felt it was not *significant.*

significantly *(adv.)*   The convict now feels that that piece of evidence would have *significantly* affected the verdict.

significance *(n.)*   A bit of evidence that was considered unimportant may turn out to be of the greatest *significance.*

Exercise 14.5: Roots and Derivatives

Fill each blank below with the root or derivative just listed that best completes the sentence.

1. Despite management's plea that it does not have the money, labor has been _____ in its demand for higher wages.

2. Management is ready to _____ that the cost of living has gone up sharply.

3. The representatives of both labor and management have at times lost their tempers; only the arbitrator has managed to remain _____.

4. When the representative of management made its first wage offer, labor said it was of no _____ and refused to consider it.

5. Labor has _____ sought a minimum salary increase of 5%.

6. Management has shown equal _____ in limiting increases to no more than 3%.

7. Labor has said it will not return to the bargaining table until management makes a _____ wage offer.

8. There is a rumor that the dispute over wages has been settled, but there is still some _____ over working conditions.

9. If wages are raised _____, there will probably be no strike.

10. Whenever a management or labor official emerges from the conference room, the reporters _____ around her or him to learn of the latest developments.

IMPROVING YOUR SPELLING: LEARNING SOME MORE HOMONYMS

Homonyms, you will recall, are words pronounced alike but different in meaning and spelling. Example: *wait,* meaning "delay," and *weight,* meaning "heaviness."

Note the spelling in these sets of homonyms:

hoarse (harsh in sound): His voice sounded *hoarse.*
horse (the animal): Get off your *horse.*

hour (sixty minutes): An *hour* went by.
our (belonging to us): Are these *our* seats?

its (belonging to it): It (the cry) reached *its* topmost note.
it's (it is): Put on warm clothes; *it's* freezing.

know (be aware of): Do you *know* how to change a tire?
no (not any): The dogs evinced *no* inclination to stray.

meat (animal flesh used as food): *Meat* is scarce.
meet (get together): Let's *meet* at the game.

pale (not bright): A *pale* light is not good for painting.
pail (bucket): Pour some water into the *pail*.

peace (opposite of war): We must live in *peace*.
piece (fragment): A *piece* of flying metal cut his hand.

seam (line formed by the sewing together of two pieces of material): The skirt is coming
   apart at the *seams*.
seem (appear): We *seem* to be riding in the wrong direction.

scene (stage setting): In the second act, there is a change of *scene*.
seen (past participle of *to see*): Have you *seen* the show?

sole (bottom of shoe): This slipper has a thin *sole*.
sole (one and only): She was the *sole* survivor.
sole (the fish): For dinner they had filet of *sole*.
soul (spirit): It might have been a lost *soul* wailing.

their (belonging to them): *Their* house has been renovated.
there (in that place): You may leave your coats *there*.
there (used before a verb): *There* were several applicants for the position.
they're (they are): *They're* after us, Bill.

Exercise 14.6: Selecting the Right Homonym
Enter the homonym required by the sentence.

1. No one lives in the house except Mrs. Wiggins; she is the _____ tenant.
   (soul, sole)

2. I was so _____ I could hardly speak. *(horse, hoarse)*

3. _____ are four quarts in a gallon. *(Their, There, They're)*

4. The _____ is nearly over. *(hour, our)*

5. There can be no _____ until the dispute is settled. *(piece, peace)*

6. A taxi was nowhere to be _____. *(scene, seen)*

7. We did not _____ what had happened. *(know, no)*

8. A person's _____ is believed to be immortal. *(sole, soul)*

9. Here is a mop and a _____. *(pale, pail)*

10. Things are not what they _____. *(seam, seem)*

11. _____ too late now to do anything about it. *(Its, It's)*

12. Who would like another _____ of pie? *(peace, piece)*

13. Can you sew a straight _____? *(seem, seam)*

14. One of my sneakers has a hole in the _____. *(soul, sole)*

15. _____ are not many things for us to talk about. *(They're, There, Their)*

16. The _____ is the breakfast room of the Day family. *(scene, seen)*

17. Please let us know when it's _____ turn. *(our, hour)*

18. The price of _____ soared last week. *(meet, meat)*

19. One of the dogs didn't get _____ fish. *(it's, its)*

20. The house was easily visible in the _____ moonlight. *(pail, pale)*

21. The dogs should be fed; _____ hungry. *(they're, their, there)*

22. She screamed herself _____. *(hoarse, horse)*

23. Do you know where we are going to _____? *(meet, meat)*

24. There was no _____ on the menu. *(sole, soul)*

25. There are plenty of seats; there is _____ waiting. *(no, know)*

STICKING TO ONE TENSE

"I took out six fish. One Ear didn't get no fish. I *come* back to the bag afterward an' got 'im his fish."

If we examine Bill's tenses, we find the following: He begins with the past tense—*took*, and continues with the past tense—*didn't get*. Then he shifts to the present tense—*come*, but ends by returning to the past tense—*got*.

Formal English does not permit us to shift tenses as Bill does. If we begin with the past tense, we must stick to the past tense; if we begin with the present, we must stick to the present.

If Jack London had wanted Bill to speak formal English, he would have written "I *came* back to the bag afterward and got him his fish." (He would also have written "One Ear didn't get *any* fish," avoiding the double negative, which likewise is not permitted in formal English.)

WRONG: The driver *stops* the bus and *told* everybody to get off.

RIGHT: The driver *stops* the bus and *tells* everybody to get off.

EXPLANATION: The first of the two parallel verbs is in the present tense—*stops*. Therefore, the second must also be in the present tense—*tells*. There is no reason to shift tenses.

WRONG: Ahead I *saw* a crowd. I *ran* over and *ask* what was wrong.

RIGHT: Ahead I *saw* a crowd. I *ran* over and *asked* what was wrong.

EXPLANATION: Since the story begins in the past tense—*saw, ran*, it should continue in the past tense—*asked.*

Exercise 14.7: Selecting the Right Tense
Enter the tense required by the sentence.

1. Just as I entered, someone _____ up and said, "Hi." *(come, came)*

2. Dee took a long lead off first and suddenly _____ toward second. *(races, raced)*

3. The president called the meeting to order. The secretary _____ the minutes. *(read, reads)*

4. Whenever I ask him to explain, he _____, "Later, not now." *(says, said)*

5. All of a sudden, she cried "Let's go!" and _____ me by the arm. *(pulled, pulls)*

6. As we turned into Pell Street, the sun _____ up. *(came, come)*

7. Darlene starts the engine and backs out the car. In a minute we _____ on the highway. *(were, are)*

8. As soon as Mom learned of our trip, she _____ to worry. *(began, begins)*

9. Play resumes and Josh _____ around right end for a seven-yard gain. *(dashed, dashes)*

10. He accused us of unfairness and _____ before we could answer. *(leaves, left)*

IMPROVING YOUR COMPOSITION SKILLS: FOLLOWING CHRONOLOGICAL ORDER

In **narration** (storytelling), authors generally use *chronological* (time) order—they give us the incidents and the details in the sequence in which they occurred in time.

When Jack London describes the howl of a wolf (page 188), he reports the details chronologically—in the exact order in which he heard them:

First Detail: A faint far cry arose on the still air.

Next Details: It soared upward with a swift rush, till it reached its topmost note, where it persisted, palpitant and tense . . .

Final Detail: and then slowly died away.

Exercise 14.8: Understanding Chronological Order

If the items in the lines below are in chronological order, write "Correct." If they are not, rewrite the entire line in the right chronological sequence. The first two answers have been entered as samples.

1. sunrise, dawn, noon, evening, midnight
   dawn, sunrise, noon, evening, midnight

2. wheel, stagecoach, railroad, radio, television
   Correct

3. winter, fall, spring, summer

4. birth, infancy, adolescence, childhood, adulthood

5. Ancient Times, Middle Ages, Renaissance, Modern Times, Future Ages

6. plan, foundation, framing, painting, roofing

7. New Year's Day, Memorial Day, Independence Day, Veterans Day, Halloween

Exercise 14.9: Describing an Incident in Chronological Order

The writer of the following paragraph did not observe chronological order. Rewrite the paragraph, using chronological order.

> **Yesterday morning, Cindy, Ralph, and I went to the beach, but by the time we got there all the good spots had been taken and we had to set up our umbrella a good distance from the water. It was mainly Carl's fault. He was supposed to be ready at 7:15, but when we called for him he was still asleep. After we had waited nearly a half hour for him to come down, his mother advised us not to wait any more and to leave without him. Because of that delay, we ran into much heavier traffic than usual, and we didn't get to the beach until 9:15.**

_____

_____

_____

_____

_____

_____

_____

_____

_____

_____

_____

_____

_____

_____

_____

_____

_____

_____

_____

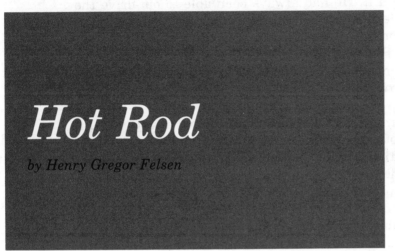

Hot Rod

by Henry Gregor Felsen

How old do you think you will be when you learn how to drive and own your first car? Bud Crayne realized both of these desires at a very tender age.

Bud Crayne was a lanky, raw-boned boy of seventeen with a long face, bold, self-confident black eyes, and a thin mouth that almost always held a challenging, reckless smile. He wore an old fedora hat with the brim turned up in front and fastened to the
5   crown with a giant safety pin, a tight fitting black leather motor-cycle jacket with zippers in the sides and sleeves and studded with metal buttons, and faded blue denim trousers. On his feet he wore short leather boots ornamented at the ankle with small brass chains.
10   Bud's parents had died when he was in grade school, and since that time he had lived with a bachelor uncle who shared furnished quarters with his young nephew. At first the housekeeper where they lived had watched over Bud, made sure he wore clean clothes and ate his meals and left for school on time. Bud's uncle didn't
15   know much about taking care of a boy, and let the housekeeper take over. As long as Bud was well and out of trouble, his uncle didn't worry.

During his early years Bud enjoyed an unusual amount of independence. The more he could look after himself, the more he
20   was allowed to. He stayed out late, roamed when and where he wished, and learned a hard kind of self-reliance.

He had started hanging around Jake Clymer's garage almost at once. Jake let him stay, taught him about cars, and paid him for his work. Bud's real interest in cars led him to spend more and

25 more time at Jake's, until, in his 'teens, he knew everything about cars that Jake could teach him, plus a good deal he'd learned himself out of books and magazines.

Bud had learned to drive while most boys were still struggling with bicycles, and once given this head start behind the wheel, he
30 never relinquished it. He had always been able to out-drive the others, and his leadership behind the wheel was seldom questioned or (any more) challenged.

At seventeen Bud was his own boss, resented any attempts by anyone to guide or counsel (he called it interfering with) his ways,
35 and he not only worked at Jake's, but practically lived at the garage.

Growing up in this way without a family, Bud always felt different from the other boys and girls in town, and was always a little apart from them. When they turned to the warmth and love
40 in their homes, he, left alone, turned to the garage, and his car. The hours that others spent with mothers, fathers, sisters or brothers, Bud spent with his homemade hop-up. It was his family. He was in the habit—like cowboys who rode lonesome ranges for isolated days at a time and talked to their horses to break the
45 silence—of talking to his car as though it were animate, and could understand, and sympathize.

His independence made him seem more mature than the other boys his age who yet had to ask parental permission to come and go. Bud regarded himself a man, and thought (he thought) like a
50 man. He had a job, and as soon as he was graduated from high school, he was going to be Jake's partner in the garage. Content with this future which assured him an income and a chance to experiment with motors, he considered himself old enough to marry. When high school was over with, and he was working full
55 time, he intended marrying LaVerne Shuler. Why not? He could support a wife, and, for the first time in his life, he would have a real home of his own.

Meanwhile, Bud worked for Jake in his free time. When he wasn't working, he was on the road. He tinkered with his car for
60 hours in order to have pleasant moments of speed on the highway. When he was behind the wheel, in control of his hopped-up motor, he was king of the road. When he was happy, his happiness reached its peak when he could express it in terms of speed and roaring power, the pull of his engine, the whistle of the wind in
65 his ears, and the glorious sensation of free flight.

When he was unhappy, discontented, moody, the wheel again offered him his answer. At these times there was solace and forgetfulness behind the wheel. The motor snarled rather than sang, speed became a lance rather than a banner, and revenge against
70 trouble was won through the conquest of other cars that accepted his challenge to race. And when he was alone on the road, his car and its speed seemed to remove him from the troubles that plagued him while his feet had contact with the earth. Once removed from bodily contact with the ground, once in motion, once in a world of

75 his own making, he escaped his troubles and sorrows in speed, in the true touch of the wheel, in the trustworthy thunder of the motor, the rushing sensation of detachment from all that was rooted or planted in earth.

UNDERSTANDING THE SELECTION

Exercise 15.1: Close Reading

In the blank space, write the *letter* of the choice that best completes the statement or answers the question.

1. The selection suggests that Bud _____.

    (A) is something of a truant
    (B) has no problems
    (C) can read well
    (D) accepts challenges, but does not challenge others

2. Bud regards advice from others _____.

    (A) as an opportunity to learn
    (B) as interference
    (C) with an open mind
    (D) with appreciation

3. The author _____.

    (A) regards Bud as a man
    (B) considers Bud old enough to marry
    (C) agrees that Bud can think like a man
    (D) suggests that Bud is lonely

4. Bud _____.

    (A) is recognized for his leadership as a driver
    (B) has learned all that he knows about cars from Jake Clymer
    (C) has been an orphan since infancy
    (D) wants to drop out of school

5. The author indicates that Bud does NOT _____.

    (A) try to escape from his trouble   (C) need revenge
    (B) enjoy speeding   (D) have a very happy life

6. Which of the following statements about the selection is UNTRUE? _____

    (A) It makes some comparisons.
    (B) It deals with Bud's life to the age of seventeen.
    (C) It observes chronological order.
    (D) It contains no dialogue.

7. The selection suggests that Bud's hop-up is LEAST important as _____.

   (A) a means of escape
   (B) a source of compensation for life's troubles
   (C) a means of transportation
   (D) a chance to excel

8. Which of the titles below would be most appropriate for the selection? _____

   (A) Growing Up
   (B) Call of the Open Road
   (C) A Difficult Childhood
   (D) Pleasures of a Hobby

LEARNING NEW WORDS

Line	Word	Meaning	Typical Use
45	**animate** *(adj.)* 'an-ə-mət	having life; living; alive	I was not the only *animate* being in the room; there were the goldfish, as well as some flies.
		(ant. **inanimate**)	This feather was once part of a living creature, but now it is *inanimate.*
51	**content** *(adj.)* kən-'tent	not disposed to complain or grumble	We wouldn't think of moving because we are very *content* with our present neighborhood.
		(ant. **discontent, discontented**)	Fred's father is going into business for himself because he is *discontented* with his job.
77	**detachment** *(n.)* di-'tach-mənt	act or process of *detaching* (separating); separation	On the road, a trailer must be securely linked to the towing vehicle to prevent *detachment.*
		(ant. **attachment**)	The stray dog developed an *attachment* for us, following us wherever we went.
1	**lanky** *(adj.)* 'laŋ-kē	awkwardly tall and thin; bony; rawboned	The *lanky* youth could not qualify as a football lineman because he lacked the necessary weight.
		(ant. **burly, husky**)	It was difficult to gain ground against our *burly* opponents, some of whom were 200 lbs. or more.

72	**plague** *(v.)* 'plāg	cause worry or distress to; vex; torment; harass	The road construction lasted two years and *plagued* drivers with dust, detours, and tie-ups.
3	**reckless** *(adj.)* 'rek-ləs	marked by a lack of caution; heedless; rash; careless	The motorist who ignored a red light and narrowly missed two cars was given a summons for *reckless* driving.
		(ant. **cautious**)	A *cautious* driver makes a complete stop at a "Full Stop" sign and checks traffic in all directions before proceeding.
30	**relinquish** *(v.)* ri-'liŋ-kwish	give up; let go of; abandon	When the librarian asked me to *relinquish* the Spanish dictionary, I got his permission to keep it ten minutes longer.
		(ant. **keep**)	
65	**sensation** *(n.)* sen-'sā-shən	feeling; awareness; consciousness produced by stimulation of the sense of sight, hearing, touch, smell, or taste	The rapid descent of the elevator gave me a *sensation* of falling.
67	**solace** *(n.)* 'säl-əs	alleviation of grief or anxiety; comfort; relief; consolation	Thank you for your cheerful "get-well" card; it was a great *solace* to me.
46	**sympathize** *(v.)* 'sim-pə-ˌthīz	1. share in suffering or grief; feel pity or compassion	I feel no pity for the reckless driver who caused the accident, but I *sympathize* with the people who were hurt.
		2. be in accord with; agree with	I *sympathize* with some of Pat's views, though I have not yet decided to vote for her.

APPLYING WHAT YOU HAVE LEARNED

Exercise 15.2: Sentence Completion

Which of the two choices correctly completes the sentence? Write the *letter* of your answer in the space provided.

1. She relinquished her seat ____.

A. and sat down

B. to an elderly passenger

2. _____ are all animate.

    A. Wood, metal, and glass
        B. Trees, grass, and birds

3. The lanky freshman _____.

    A. towers above his companions
        B. is thirty pounds overweight

4. Most people are inclined to sympathize with the _____ fortunate.

    A. more
        B. less

5. The team has been plagued by a long string of _____.

    A. victories
        B. injuries

6. If you are content, why do you look so _____?

    A. hurt
        B. pleased

7. Though your team lost, the fact that you _____ should give you some solace.

    A. scored two touchdowns
        B. dropped the ball at the goal line

8. The reckless camper _____.

    A. cooked the evening meal over an outdoor grill
        B. threw a lighted match into the brush

9. There is no sensation in _____.

    A. the limb of a dead tree
        B. a bear cub's paw

10. Detachment of the stub is simple: just _____ on the dotted line.

    A. sign your name
        B. tear it off

Exercise 15.3: Definitions

Each expression below defines a word taught on pages 204–205. Enter that word in the space provided.

_____ **1.** awkwardly tall and thin

_____ **2.** let go of

_____ **3.** act or process of separating

_____ **4.** share in suffering or grief

_____ **5.** marked by lack of caution

_____ **6.** alleviation of grief or anxiety

_____ **7.** having life

_____ **8.** consciousness produced by stimulation of a sense

_____ **9.** cause worry or distress to

_____ **10.** not disposed to complain or grumble

Exercise 15.4: Synonyms and Antonyms

Fill the blanks in column A with the required synonyms and antonyms, selecting them from column B.

	Column A	*Column B*
_____	**1.** antonym for *pleased*	sympathize
_____	**2.** synonym for *feel pity*	alive
_____	**3.** antonym for *keep*	plague
_____	**4.** synonym for *vex*	reckless
_____	**5.** antonym for *burly*	discontented
_____	**6.** synonym for *feeling*	detachment
_____	**7.** antonym for *cautious*	sensation
_____	**8.** antonym for *inanimate*	solace
_____	**9.** synonym for *separation*	relinquish
_____	**10.** synonym for *relief*	lanky

LEARNING SOME ROOTS AND DERIVATIVES

Each word in bold type is a *root*. The words below it are its *derivatives*.

animate *(adj.)*	The figure appeared to be a statue, but when it moved slightly, I knew it was *animate*.
animate *(v.)*	By asking an interesting question, you can *animate* a lifeless discussion.
animation *(n.)*	Your voice lacks liveliness. Put some *animation* into it.
content *(adj.)*	Peter was not *content* with his seat and asked the teacher to change it.
content *(v.)*	The teacher told Peter that, since she was busy, he would have to *content* himself with his assigned seat for a while.
contentment *(n.)*	Later, when she changed his seat, she could tell by his look of *contentment* that he was pleased.

detach *(v.)*	This coat has an extra lining for added warmth. It is easy to *detach*.
detachable *(adj.)*	The lining is *detachable*.
detachment *(n.)*	*Detachment* of the lining is no problem—simply zip it out.
plague *(n.)*	The *plague*, a deadly disease, killed millions of people during the Middle Ages.
plague *(v.)*	"These debts *plague* me," said the shopkeeper. "I wish I could find a way to pay them off."
reckless *(adj.)*	Becoming *reckless*, Rita raced across the traffic on Main Street, against the light.
recklessly *(adv.)*	She *recklessly* dodged one car after another to get to the other side of the street.
recklessness *(n.)*	Such *recklessness* sometimes results in a fatal accident.
solace *(n.)*	It was good to hear you say that you thought I should have been given the prize. Your words were a *solace* to me.
solace *(v.)*	Your kind words did much to *solace* me when I was feeling blue.
sympathy *(n.)*	In the coming election, Dad is going to vote for the Republicans, but Mother's *sympathy* is with the Democrats.
sympathetic *(adj.)*	Mother is *sympathetic* toward the views of the Democratic Party.
sympathetically *(adv.)*	Dad is *sympathetically* inclined toward the Republican Party platform.
sympathize *(v.)*	Mother *sympathizes* with the Democrats.
sympathizer *(n.)*	Dad is a Republican *sympathizer*.

Exercise 15.5: Roots and Derivatives

Fill each blank below with the root or derivative just listed that best completes the sentence.

1. The bag has a(n) _____ shoulder strap that is very easy to take off or put back.

2. In the first inning, Tom pitched _____, walking three batters and making four wild pitches.

3. Jane wants the Bears to win, but I am a Red Sox _____.

4. The moral of the story is that sudden wealth may bring unhappiness instead of

    _____.

5. Yesterday you seemed lifeless, but today you are full of _____.

6. If you visit patients too soon after their surgery, you may annoy them rather than

_____ them.

7. Most parents contribute to the Scholarship Fund because of their _____

with its goals.

8. Today we have the medical knowledge to deal effectively with any outbreak of the

_____ .

9. Our English teacher has a wonderful sense of humor, and he uses it to

_____ his lessons.

10. Some people can never be satisfied; nothing will _____ them.

IMPROVING YOUR SPELLING: PROBLEMS OF FINAL -Y

I. Attaching Suffixes

A. Look at the letter before final -Y. If it is a *consonant*, change the Y to I before attaching the suffix.

> marry + ED = married
> happy + NESS = happiness

B. However, do not change the -Y if the suffix begins with an I.

> marry + ING = marrying

C. If the letter before final -Y is a *vowel*, do not change the Y.

> play + ED = played
> enjoy + ABLE = enjoyable

D. Note that adding ED to *lay, pay, say,* and their compounds results in *laid, paid, said, mislaid, repaid, unsaid,* etc.

> lay + ED = laid
> pay + ED = paid

E. Note, too, that *day + ly = daily.*

> day + LY = daily

II. Forming Plurals

A. Look at the letter before final -Y. If it is a *vowel*, simply add the suffix S.

> turkey + S = turkeys
> highway + S = highways

B. If the letter before final -Y is a **consonant,** change the Y to I and add the suffix ES.

    lady + ES = ladies
    family + ES = families

Exercise 15.6: Attaching Suffixes to Words Ending in *Y*
Fill in the blanks.

  1. unhappy + est   = _____

  2. employ + able   = _____

  3. plural of *key*   = _____

  4. boy + ish   = _____

  5. destroy + ed   = _____

  6. plural of *city*   = _____

  7. fry + ed   = _____

  8. worry + ing   = _____

  9. plural of *delay*   = _____

10. early + er   = _____

11. overlay + ed   = _____

12. plural of *attorney*   = _____

13. employ + ment   = _____

14. lobby + ist   = _____

15. plural of *liberty*   = _____

16. stay + ed   = _____

17. underpay + ed   = _____

18. plural of *ally*   = _____

19. plural of *company*   = _____

20. day + ly   = _____

Exercise 15.7: Removing Suffixes
Fill in the blanks.

  1. grayish − ish   = _____

  2. hurried − ed   = _____

  3. singular of *alleys*   = _____

  4. prepaid − ed   = _____

  5. terrifying − ing   = _____

6. singular of *necessities* = _____

7. delayed − ed = _____

8. bodily − ly = _____

9. singular of *landladies* = _____

10. lonelier − er = _____

SOME EXPRESSIONS TO AVOID

The verb *graduate* is usually followed by *from:*

"He had a job, and as soon as he was *graduated from* high school, he was going to be Jake's partner in the garage."

1. AVOID: My brother *graduated* high school.
   SAY: My brother *graduated from* high school.
   OR SAY: My brother *was graduated from* high school.

The adjective *different* is usually followed by *from,* rather than *than:*

". . . Bud always felt *different from* the other boys . . ."

2. AVOID: Astronomy is *different than* astrology.
   SAY: Astronomy is *different from* astrology.

Here are some further expressions for you to avoid.

3. AVOID: The game will be played *irregardless* of the weather.
   SAY: The game will be played *regardless* of the weather.

4. AVOID: Please get *off of* the field.
   SAY: Please get *off* the field.

5. AVOID: Ira is six *foot* tall.
   SAY: Ira is six *feet* tall.

6. AVOID: *Me and my friend* had a quarrel.
   SAY: *My friend and I* had a quarrel.

7. AVOID: You should *try and* do better.
   SAY: You should *try to* do better.

8. AVOID: The *reason* is *because* I was sick.
   SAY: The *reason* is *that* I was sick.

9. AVOID: We had a *real* good time.
   SAY: We had a *really* good time.

10. AVOID: *This here* book is all about hockey.
    SAY: *This* book is all about hockey.

Exercise 15.8: Proofreading to Improve Usage

If the sentence is incorrect, rewrite it correctly in the space provided. If the sentence is correct, write "Correct." (Two of the sentences are correct.)

1. After failing Spanish, Nora promised she would try and do better.

   _____

2. The reason is that we had a flat tire.

   _____

3. If you need something, buy it irregardless of the cost.

   _____

4. Your answer is different than mine.

   _____

5. When did your sister graduate high school?

   _____

6. She is five feet tall and has brown hair.

   _____

7. Kindly take your feet off of that chair.

   _____

8. That was a real good book.

   _____

9. This here pie is delicious.

   _____

10. Me and my brother get along well.

   _____

IMPROVING YOUR COMPOSITION SKILLS: KNOWING WHEN TO BEGIN A NEW PARAGRAPH

A *paragraph* is a group of sentences dealing with one topic. Turn now to page 201 and reread lines 1–17 of the selection from *Hot Rod*.

Question: Why does the author begin a new paragraph in line 10?

Answer: He has come to a new topic.

The first paragraph (lines 1–9) deals with Bud's appearance. All the sentences in the paragraph are on that topic.

After line 9, the author has no more to say about Bud's appearance. He is ready to start a new paragraph.

The second paragraph (lines 10–17) deals with Bud's upbringing after the death of his parents. All the sentences in the second paragraph deal with this topic.

Summary: A paragraph is a group of sentences dealing with one topic. When you come to a new topic, begin a new paragraph.

Dividing a Piece of Writing Into Paragraphs

The following would be more effective if divided into two paragraphs. Read it. Then do the exercise below.

> **Ben Franklin, tenth son of a candlemaker, was born in Boston on January 17, 1706. He left school after two years to help his father. Ben, who loved reading, hated candlemaking, and his father worried about what to do with him. James Franklin, Ben's half-brother, was already doing well. Only nine years older, James was a printer and the editor of a newspaper. James was therefore persuaded to take Ben in as an apprentice.**

Exercise 15.9: Beginning a New Paragraph

Write your answers to the following questions in the spaces provided:

1. What sentence in the above paragraph about Ben Franklin should begin a new paragraph? Write that sentence.

   _____

2. Why should the sentence you have chosen begin a new paragraph?

   _____

   _____

The Old Curiosity Shop

by Charles Dickens

Were you ever lost? Did you ever try to help someone who was lost?
   Late one night many, many years ago in the city of London, a pretty little girl who had lost her way stops a stranger to ask for directions.

One night I had roamed into the City, and was walking slowly on in my usual way, musing upon a great many things, when I was arrested by an inquiry, the purport of which did not reach me, but which seemed to be addressed to myself, and was proffered in
5 a soft sweet voice that struck me very pleasantly. I turned hastily round and found at my elbow a pretty little girl, who begged to be directed to a certain street at a considerable distance, and indeed in quite another quarter of the town.

"It's a very long way from here," said I, "my child."

10 "I know that, Sir," she replied timidly. "I am afraid it is a very long way, for I came from there tonight."

"Alone?" said I, in some surprise.

"Oh yes, I don't mind that, but I am a little frightened now, for I had lost my road."

15 "And what made you ask it of me? Suppose I should tell you wrong."

"I am sure you will not do that," said the little creature; "you are such a very old gentleman, and walk so slow yourself."

I cannot describe how much I was impressed by this appeal
20 and the energy with which it was made, which brought a tear into the child's clear eye, and made her slight figure tremble as she looked up into my face.

"Come," said I, "I'll take you there."

She put her hand in mine as confidingly as if she had known
me from her cradle, and we trudged away together: the little creature accommodating her pace to mine, and rather seeming to lead
and take care of me than I to be protecting her. I observed that
every now and then she stole a curious look at my face as if to
make quite sure that I was not deceiving her, and that these
glances (very sharp and keen they were too) seemed to increase
her confidence at every repetition.

For my part, my curiosity and interest were at least equal to
the child's, for child she certainly was, although I thought it probable from what I could make out, that her very small and delicate
frame imparted a peculiar youthfulness to her appearance.
Though more scantily attired than she might have been, she was
dressed with perfect neatness, and betrayed no marks of poverty
or neglect.

"Who has sent you so far by yourself?" said I.

"Somebody who is very kind to me, Sir."

"And what have you been doing?"

"That, I must not tell," said the child firmly.

There was something in the manner of this reply which caused
me to look at the little creature with an involuntary expression of
surprise; for I wondered what kind of errand it might be that occa-
sioned her to be prepared for questioning. Her quick eye seemed
to read my thoughts, for as it met mine she added that there was
no harm in what she had been doing, but it was a great secret—a
secret which she did not even know herself.

This was said with no appearance of cunning or deceit, but
with an unsuspicious frankness that bore the impress of truth.

UNDERSTANDING THE SELECTION

Exercise 16.1: Close Reading

In the blank space, write the *letter* of the choice that best completes the statement or
answers the question.

1. The narrator _____.

   (A) first notices the child when she tugs at his elbow
   (B) hears the child's voice before he sees her
   (C) sees the child before she sees him
   (D) seems to be hard of hearing

2. The child _____.

   (A) is completely without fear
   (B) walks more slowly than the narrator

(C) appears highly intelligent

(D) hesitates before answering questions

3. The narrator _____.

(A) suspects that the child is lying

(B) is not used to walking slowly

(C) is not surprised that the child has made a long trip by herself

(D) seems to know his way around town

4. When asked what she has been doing, the child _____.

(A) indicates she has not been doing anything wrong

(B) tells all she knows

(C) remains silent

(D) invents an obvious lie

5. The word *betrayed,* as used in the selection on line 37 ("she was dressed with perfect neatness, and *betrayed* no marks of poverty or neglect"), means _____.

(A) treacherously disclosed

(B) concealed

(C) showed

(D) covered up

6. The narrator's attitude toward the child includes all the following EXCEPT _____.

(A) surprise

(B) suspicion

(C) concern

(D) admiration

7. Which of the following statements is UNTRUE? _____

(A) The child observes the narrator closely.

(B) The selection makes little use of dialogue.

(C) The narrator observes the child closely.

(D) The child makes no attempt to suppress her true feelings.

8. The selection offers no specific information about any of the following EXCEPT _____.

(A) the thoughts of the characters

(B) the destination of the pedestrians

(C) the date of the incident

(D) the names and ages of the characters

LEARNING NEW WORDS

Line	Word	Meaning	Typical Use
26	**accommodate** *(v.)* ə-'käm-ə-ˌdāt	1. adapt; adjust; make fit	When we moved, it did not take me long to *accommodate* myself to my new school.
		2. have space for; hold without crowding; contain	The new hotel can *accommodate* two hundred guests.
19	**appeal** *(n.)* ə-'pēl	earnest request; plea; call for help	Dozens of volunteers responded to the hospital's *appeal* for blood donors.
36	**attire** *(v.)* ə-'tī(ə)r	put garments on; clothe; dress	On special occasions like graduations and weddings, people *attire* themselves in their very best clothes.
31	**confidence** *(n.)* 'kän-fəd-ən(t)s	feeling of trust; faith; reliance	You may have *confidence* in what my brother has promised, for he always keeps his word.
		(ant. **doubt, apprehension***)*	I have no *apprehension* about lending my science notes to Selma, as I have absolute trust in her.
32	**curiosity** *(n.)* ˌkyùr-ē-'äs-ət-ē	1. eager desire to know; inquisitiveness	You can satisfy your *curiosity* about Lauren's absence by calling her and asking why she has not been in school.
		2. strange or rare object; article valued for its strangeness or rarity	There are many people who visit antique shops in search of *curiosities*.
50	**deceit** *(n.)* di-'sēt	act of *deceiving* (misleading); dishonest trick; cheating; lying	Wise dealers treat their customers fairly because they know that in the long run *deceit* does not pay.
		(ant. **honesty***)*	
34	**delicate** *(adj.)* 'del-i-kət	easily hurt or damaged; weak; frail; sickly	If you drop your watch, you will almost certainly damage it, as it has a very *delicate* mechanism.

51	**frankness** *(n.)* 'fraŋk-nəs	openness and honesty in expressing what one thinks; outspokenness	I appreciate your *frankness* in telling me that this jacket does not fit me. It's good to know the truth, even if it hurts.
		(ant. **reticence, silence**)	Some of my friends said nothing when they saw me in this jacket, and by their *reticence* they led me to believe that it looks good on me.
44	**involuntary** *(adj.)* (')in-'väl-ən-ˌter-ē	not subject to control by the will; automatic; instinctive	We cannot stop a sneeze or a yawn because they are *involuntary* acts.
		(ant. **voluntary**)	My decision to quit was entirely *voluntary;* I left because I wanted to.
10	**timidly** *(adv.)* 'tim-əd-lē	in a *timid* (fearful) manner; fearfully; shyly; hesitantly	When it seemed that there might be a fight, most of the bystanders *timidly* withdrew to safe ground.
		(ant. **valiantly, courageously**)	One stranger, however, *valiantly* remained on the scene in an attempt to get both sides to talk things over.

APPLYING WHAT YOU HAVE LEARNED

Exercise 16.2: Sentence Completion

Which of the two choices correctly completes the sentence? Write the *letter* of your answer in the space provided.

1. ____ is usually an involuntary remark.

    A. "O.K."   B. "Ouch!"

2. To ____ is to practice deceit.

    A. pretend to be older than you are   B. come late to a quiz

3. The manager was attired ____.

    A. after a long day   B. in a business suit

4. An ____ is an appeal with which most of us are familiar.

    A. S.O.S.   B. I.O.U.

5. I was ____ to follow the path as my eyes accommodated themselves to the dark.

    A. unable   B. able

6. If you behave timidly, others may think you are ____.

    A. rude   B. scared

7. Her curiosity shows that she is ____.

    A. eager to learn   B. not interested

8. A ____ is extremely delicate.

    A. spider's web   B. mountaintop

9. George must have confidence in you, for he ____.

    A. gave you the combination to his locker   B. has never borrowed a thing from you

10. The child's frankness ____.

    A. prevented us from learning the secret   B. helped us to get at the facts

Exercise 16.3: Definitions

Each expression below defines a word taught on pages 217–218. Enter that word in the space provided.

_____ **1.** feeling of trust

_____ **2.** have space for

_____ **3.** openness in expressing what one thinks

_____ **4.** in a fearful manner

_____ **5.** easily hurt or damaged

_____ **6.** put garments on

_____ **7.** not subject to control by the will

_____ **8.** eager desire to know

_____ **9.** call for help

_____ **10.** act of misleading

Exercise 16.4: Synonyms and Antonyms

Fill the blanks in column A with the required synonyms and antonyms, selecting them from column B.

	Column A	Column B
_____	1. antonym for *apprehension*	delicate
_____	2. synonym for *frail*	voluntary
_____	3. antonym for *valiantly*	appeal
_____	4. synonym for *adjust*	confidence
_____	5. antonym for *honesty*	attire
_____	6. synonym for *plea*	accommodate
_____	7. antonym for *reticence*	timidly
_____	8. synonym for *clothe*	curiosity
_____	9. antonym for *instinctive*	frankness
_____	10. synonym for *inquisitiveness*	deceit

LEARNING SOME ROOTS AND DERIVATIVES

Each word in bold type is a *root*. The words below it are its *derivatives*.

accommodate *(v.)* The Seaside Inn can *accommodate* eighty-four guests.

accommodation *(n.)* The Seaside Inn has *accommodations* for eighty-four guests.

appeal *(n.)* If found guilty, a defendant may make an *appeal* to a higher tribunal.

appeal *(v.)* If found guilty, a defendant may *appeal* to a higher court.

attire *(v.)* It makes no sense to *attire* yourself in your best clothes to do a cleaning job.

attire *(n.)* People generally wear their best *attire* to a wedding.

confide *(v.)* Defendants must *confide* in their lawyers. Whom else are they to trust?

confident *(adj.)* Defendants have to feel *confident* that their lawyers will not let them down.

confidently *(adv.)* They should *confidently* tell their lawyers everything, without fear that they will be betrayed.

confidential (adj.)	He should have so much trust in his lawyer as to be able to give him the most *confidential* information.
confidentially (adv.)	He should be able to tell his attorney *confidentially* things that he would tell to no one else.
confidence (n.)	A defendant must have *confidence* in his lawyer.
curious (adj.)	Peter showed no interest in the seashell, but Sally was *curious* about it.
curiously (adv.)	She examined the shell *curiously*.
curiosity (n.)	Her *curiosity* prompted her to look up seashells in the encyclopedia.
deceive (v.)	Why do you suspect Stan of lying? What reason can he have to *deceive* you?
deceiver (n.)	He has always told the truth. He is not a *deceiver*.
deceit (n.)	I have never known him to practice *deceit*.
deceitful (adj.)	I have never known Stan to be *deceitful*.
deceitfully (adv.)	If he did misinform you, he must have done it accidentally, not *deceitfully*.
deception (n.)	I cannot believe that Stan would be guilty of *deception*.
delicate (adj.)	This camera is a *delicate* instrument. Handle it with care.
delicately (adv.)	This camera may break if dropped. It is *delicately* constructed.
delicacy (n.)	Use extreme caution in handling equipment of such *delicacy*.
frank (adj.)	Since you have asked me to be *frank*, I must tell you that you are selfish.
frankly (adv.)	I tell you *frankly* that, if you do not change, you will lose all your friends, including me.
frankness (n.)	My *frankness* may hurt you, but you have asked for the truth, and I have given it to you.
involuntary (adj.)	My eyes blink when a flashbulb goes off. It is an *involuntary* reaction.
involuntarily (adv.)	My eyes blink *involuntarily* when a flashbulb goes off.
timid (adj.)	Jump in. The water can't hurt you. Don't be *timid*.
timidly (adv.)	Don't stand so *timidly* at the edge of the pool. The water is fine. Jump in.
timidity (n.)	I, too, was once afraid of the water, but I got over my *timidity*. You can, too.

Exercise 16.5: Roots and Derivatives

Fill each blank below with the root or derivative just listed that best completes the sentence.

1. Are they telling the truth, or are they trying to _____ us?

2. Gossips are _____ about other people's business.

3. I walked up to the microphone _____; I was scared.

4. Motel after motel flashed the "No Vacancy" sign; it was very hard to find a(n) _____.

5. Let me ask you to be perfectly _____ and not to hold back any information.

6. My teeth chattered _____; it was so cold!

7. Pictures will be taken at the wedding; wear your best _____.

8. Ed's health is of such _____ that he will have to remain at home for at least another month.

9. What I have told you is not _____; you may reveal it to anyone you wish.

10. Should our expenses continue to go up, we shall have to _____ to our members for an increase in dues.

IMPROVING YOUR SPELLING: SOME TROUBLESOME DERIVATIVES

A few derivatives are difficult to spell because they unexpectedly drop or change one or two letters present in the root.

ROOT	DERIVATIVE	
curio<u>u</u>s	curio<u>s</u>ity	(<u>u</u> dropped)
genero<u>u</u>s	genero<u>s</u>ity	(<u>u</u> dropped)
fo<u>u</u>r	fo<u>r</u>ty	(<u>u</u> dropped) Note, however: fo<u>u</u>rteen, fo<u>u</u>rth.
den<u>o</u>unce	den<u>u</u>nciation	(<u>o</u> dropped)
pron<u>o</u>unce	pron<u>u</u>nciation	(<u>o</u> dropped)
court<u>eou</u>s	court<u>e</u>sy	(<u>ou</u> dropped)
argu<u>e</u>	argu<u>m</u>ent	(<u>e</u> dropped)
aw<u>e</u>	aw<u>f</u>ul	(<u>e</u> dropped)
disast<u>e</u>r	disast<u>r</u>ous	(<u>e</u> dropped)

enter	entrance	(e dropped)
hinder	hindrance	(e dropped)
monster	monstrous	(e dropped)
nine	ninth	(e dropped) Note, however: nineteen, ninety.
proceed	procedure	(e dropped)
remember	remembrance	(e dropped)
detain	detention	(ai becomes e)
maintain	maintenance	(ai becomes e)
retain	retention	(ai becomes e)
prevail	prevalent	(i dropped)
till	until	(l dropped)

Exercise 16.6: Attaching a Suffix to a Root

Fill the blanks in column C. Follow the sample:

	(A)	(B)	(C)
	Root	*+ Suffix*	*= Derivative*
	disaster	+ ous	= **disastrous**
1.	four	+ ty	= _____
2.	nine	+ ty	= _____
3.	generous	+ ity	= _____
4.	maintain	+ ance	= _____
5.	courteous	+ y	= _____
6.	nine	+ th	= _____
7.	four	+ th	= _____
8.	enter	+ ance	= _____
9.	awe	+ ful	= _____
10.	prevail	+ ent	= _____

Exercise 16.7: Tracing a Derivative to Its Root

Fill the blanks in column B.

(A) *Derivative*	(B) *Root*
pronunciation	**pronounce**

1. hindrance   _____

2. until   _____

3. detention   _____

4. awful   _____

5. curiosity   _____

6. procedure   _____

7. denunciation   _____

8. argument   _____

9. remembrance   _____

10. retention   _____

USING COMPOUND SUBJECTS

1. A **compound subject** (a subject consisting of two or more words connected by *and*) usually takes a plural verb.

> "For my part, my <u>curiosity and interest</u> <u>were</u> (not *was*) at least equal to the child's . . ."

> <u>Milk, butter, and cheese</u> <u>need</u> (not *needs*) to be kept in the refrigerator.

2. However, use a singular verb if the two words in the compound subject refer to the same person or thing.

> The <u>owner and operator</u> of the vehicle <u>is</u> (not *are*) Chester A. Banks.

> The <u>capital and largest city</u> of Massachusetts <u>is</u> (not *are*) Boston.

3. Also, use a singular verb if the compound subject is considered as a single thing, rather than two distinct things.

> <u>Spaghetti and meatballs</u> <u>was</u> not on the menu.
> (*Spaghetti and meatballs* is a single dish.)

> <u>Law and order</u> <u>has</u> to be maintained at all costs.
> (*Law and order* is a single idea.)

Exercise 16.8: Selecting the Verb for a Compound Subject

Each sentence below has a compound subject. Select the verb for that subject and write it in the blank space.

1. Radio and television *(help, helps)* _____ to keep us informed.
2. The patient's pulse and temperature *(has, have)* _____ been normal all day.
3. Ham and eggs *(is, are)* _____ served at breakfast.
4. When *(is, are)* _____ Paul and Eric leaving?
5. The winner and new champion *(was, were)* _____ acclaimed at the end of the bout.
6. Abraham and Straus *(is, are)* _____ a leading department store.
7. Your work and conduct *(needs, need)* _____ improvement.
8. The sum and substance of the matter *(is, are)* _____ that we are running out of cash.
9. Macaroni and cheese *(is, are)* _____ today's luncheon special.
10. Bud's speed and experience *(makes, make)* _____ him our most valuable player.

IMPROVING YOUR COMPOSITION SKILLS: USING DIALOGUE THAT REVEALS CHARACTER

Dialogue (conversation) can bring a piece of writing to life because it often tells us a great deal about people. We have seen this in the bits of dialogue that Dickens uses so effectively to reveal the character of the little girl and the old gentleman in the selection on pages 214–215.

Exercise 16.9: Using Dialogue in Reporting an Incident

Describe an incident that includes a brief amount of dialogue—especially dialogue that reveals character. Use no more than about a hundred words.

Hints for Topics:

You ask someone—a stranger or a person you know—for directions, information, or assistance.

Someone—a stranger or a person you know—offers to sell you something or asks you for a contribution.

Sample Incident

As my friend and I were eating our lunch in a downtown restaurant last Saturday, a well-dressed young man we had never seen before approached and put an expensive-looking bracelet on our table.

"It's real gold, honest. I'll sell it to you very cheap. It's a beauty. You wouldn't believe how little I'm asking.

"Sorry," I said, speaking for my friend and myself. "We're not interested."

Another Sample Incident

I was standing in the bus, and I really wanted to sit down because I had been on my feet a long time, waiting for the bus to come. Hoping to find a seat at the rear, I worked my way down the aisle. Sure enough, there was a vacant seat taken up with somebody's belongings—a gym bag, a tennis racket, and some other things.

"Is this seat taken?" I asked courteously, addressing the person to whom they seemed to belong.

"Can't you see it is?" said the owner. "What do you want me to do with all these things?"

Now describe your incident.

_____

_____

_____

_____

_____

_____

_____

_____

_____

_____

_____

_____

Review IV.1: Vocabulary and Spelling

Fill in the missing letters of the words at the right of the definition. Then write the complete word in the blank space.

	DEFINITION	WORD	COMPLETE WORD
1.	not subject to control by the will	INVOLUN __ __ __ __	_____
2.	grow dim	__ __ DE	_____
3.	hold without crowding	ACC __ __ __ __ DATE	_____
4.	number of similar things grouped together	__ __ __ STER	_____
5.	feel pity or compassion	SYM __ __ __ __ IZE	_____
6.	heavy of body	__ __ __ TLY	_____
7.	conclude from known facts	DED __ __ __	_____
8.	pass through or over	__ __ __ VERSE	_____
9.	act of separating	DE __ __ __ __ MENT	_____
10.	eager desire to know	__ __ __ IOSITY	_____
11.	quarrel over petty things	BIC __ __ __	_____
12.	become worn or ragged	__ __ AY	_____
13.	call for help	PL __ __	_____
14.	cause worry or distress to	__ __ __ GUE	_____
15.	hand-operated	MAN __ __ __	_____
16.	being the only one of its kind	__ NIQ __ __	_____
17.	move upward	SO __ __	_____
18.	not disposed to grumble	__ __ __ TENT	_____
19.	easily damaged	DELIC __ __ __	_____
20.	alleviation of grief	__ __ LACE	_____

Review IV.2: Synonyms

To each line below, add a word that has the *same meaning* as the first two words on the line. Choose your words from the vocabulary list below.

1. clothe; dress _____
2. awareness; feeling _____
3. tale; story _____
4. patron; customer _____
5. coolly; calmly _____
6. rash; heedless _____
7. show; reveal _____
8. alive; living _____
9. consequence; importance _____
10. embellishment; decoration _____

Vocabulary List

evince	client
significance	narrative
ornament	attire
animate	dispassionately
sensation	reckless

Review IV.3: Antonyms

For each italicized word in Column A, write the best *antonym* from Column B.

	Column A	*Column B*
_____	1. will probably *desist*	relinquish
_____	2. the *burly* doorman	commonplace
_____	3. proceeded *valiantly*	frankness
_____	4. a *lowly* public servant	confidence
_____	5. *deny* the fact	persist
_____	6. an *extraordinary* event	timidly
_____	7. complete *reticence*	honestly
_____	8. *keep* everything	lanky
_____	9. deal *deceitfully*	acknowledge
_____	10. a feeling of *apprehension*	pompous

Review IV.4: Removal of Prefixes and Suffixes

From the derivative in column A, remove the prefix and/or suffix in column B, and write the root word in column C. Study the three examples that follow.

Column A		Column B		Column C
(DERIVATIVE)	−	(PREFIX and/or SUFFIX)	=	(ROOT WORD)
incompatible	−	in	=	**compatible**
generosity	−	ity	=	**generous**
displacement	−	dis *and* ment	=	**place**

	Column A		Column B		Column C
1.	inanimate	−	in	=	_____
2.	accommodation	−	ion	=	_____
3.	unhappiness	−	un *and* ness	=	_____
4.	curiosity	−	ity	=	_____
5.	dispassionate	−	dis *and* ate	=	_____
6.	remembrance	−	ance	=	_____
7.	confidence	−	ence	=	_____
8.	impatiently	−	im *and* ly	=	_____
9.	reducible	−	ible	=	_____
10.	portliness	−	ness	=	_____

Review IV.5: Wordbuilding With Suffixes

To the root in column A, add the suffix in column B, and write the derivative in column C. Study the sample.

Column A		Column B		Column C
(ROOT)	+	(SUFFIX)	=	(DERIVATIVE)
curious	+	ity	=	**curiosity**

	Column A		Column B		Column C
1.	maintain	+	ance	=	_____
2.	argue	+	ment	=	_____
3.	courteous	+	y	=	_____
4.	nine	+	teen	=	_____
5.	disaster	+	ous	=	_____
6.	four	+	ty	=	_____
7.	prevail	+	ent	=	_____
8.	generous	+	ity	=	_____
9.	detain	+	tion	=	_____
10.	proceed	+	ure	=	_____

Review IV.6: Homonyms
Insert the correct choice.

1. Can you ride a _____ (hoarse, horse)?
2. Flounder, salmon, and _____ (soul, sole) are in good supply.
3. Where shall we _____ (meat, meet)?
4. The dog raised _____ (it's, its) ears.
5. Will you be _____ (they're, their, there)?

Review IV.7: Problems of Words Ending in Y
Fill in the blanks.

1. pay + ment = _____
2. plural of *necessity* = _____
3. burly + er = _____
4. singular of *enemies* = _____
5. gloomy + est = _____
6. plural of *bay* = _____
7. hurry + ing = _____
8. repay + ed = _____
9. plural of *alley* = _____
10. baby + ish = _____

Review IV.8: Sentence Completion
Complete each sentence below with the most appropriate word from the following vocabulary list.

Vocabulary List

commonplace	content	confidence
attire	unique	appeal
soar	sympathize	relinquish
evince	animate	bicker

1. I _____ with the losers. Don't you feel sorry for them, too?

2. We thought the guests would like the flowers, but they did not _____ any enthusiasm for them.

3. Why don't you have _____ in the dean? Everybody else trusts her.

4. In walked Jeffrey, all dressed up in his finest holiday _____.

5. Let's not _____ about the batting order. You can bat first, if you insist.

6. Andrea was not _____; everyone else seemed satisfied.

7. Scoring the highest mark has become _____ for Russ. He does it all the time.

8. When Dr. Goodman got on the crowded bus, I thought I should _____ my seat to her.

9. It was long believed that there is life on the moon, but no _____ creatures have been found there.

10. You will not find another player like Connie anywhere; she is _____.

Review IV.9: Roots and Derivatives
On lines B and C, write the required forms of the italicized word on line A.

1. A. We thought you were honest, not *deceitful.*
   B. We never expected you to _____ us.
   C. Who would have guessed that you could be such a sly _____?

2. A. Motorists may lose much more than their licenses if they drive *recklessly.*
   B. _____ drivers may lose their lives.
   C. Overcome your _____.

3. A. Drivers who keep breaking traffic laws and get hurt shouldn't expect any *sympathy.*
   B. No one will be _____.
   C. We _____ with the innocent victims.

4. A. Some people always complain. Nothing can *content* them.
   B. They can never find peace and _____.
   C. They will never be _____.

5. A. Don't try to spare my feelings. Be *frank.*
   B. Speak _____.
   C. I prefer _____.

6. A. Our meetings are conducted simply—without *pomp.*
   B. The president of the club does not insist on being addressed _____ as "Madam President."
   C. She thinks that _____ titles are out of place in the club.

7. A. The information you give physicians is *confidential;* they will not reveal it to anyone else without your permission.

B. You may _____ in your physician.

C. You may have _____ in your physician.

8. A. Monica is good in *narration*.

   B. When she tells a story, everybody listens. She is a skillful _____.

   C. She knows how to _____.

9. A. Does your little brother bother you *persistently*?

   B. It is hard to put up with _____ nagging.

   C. If my brother were to _____ in making a nuisance of himself, I wouldn't stand for it.

10. A. A doorknob makes it possible for us to open and close a door. It also serves as *ornamentation*.

    B. A well-designed metal knob adds beauty to a wooden door; it is an attractive _____.

    C. Doorknobs have both practical and _____ uses.

11. A. Don't be *timid*. There is nothing to be afraid of.

    B. The dog won't bite you. Don't act so _____.

    C. Get rid of your _____.

12. A. When Santa Claus emerged from the helicopter, the children eyed him *curiously*.

    B. They gave him _____ glances.

    C. They observed him with _____.

13. A. Though Sharon is a talented skater, she knows she is not *unique*.

    B. She does not claim to be _____ talented; she acknowledges that others may skate as well, or even better.

    C. She makes no claim to _____.

14. A. A gain of 25% is *significant*.

    B. A gain of 5% does not usually mean much, but an improvement of 25% has real _____.

    C. Your marks have improved _____ since our last talk.

15. A. The student actors were lifeless; they did not seem *animate*.

    B. What can we do to _____ their acting?

    C. How can we put some _____ into the play?

16. A. The patient's health is of such *delicacy* that he is not permitted to have too many visitors.

    B. When I greeted him, he smiled so _____ that it was obvious to me that he was still weak.

C. The patient is in _____ health.

17. A. My winter jacket has a *detachable* hood.

   B. On warm days, I _____ the hood.

   C. _____ is easy; the hood zips out. Attachment is more difficult.

18. A. Marie is *confident* that she can win the election.

   B. She _____ expects to be declared the winner.

   C. She has a great deal of self-_____.

19. A. From their investigation, the detectives have been able to *deduce* that the thief must have known the combination to the safe.

   B. Also _____ is the fact that the burglar must have worn gloves; there were no fingerprints.

   C. The detectives are going over the evidence to see if any further _____ can be made.

20. A. If I could vote, I would cast my ballot for Simpson. I am *sympathetically* inclined to his views.

   B. My _____ is with Simpson.

   C. I am a Simpson _____.

Review IV.10: Concise Writing

Rewrite the following 120-word paragraph in the space provided, keeping all its ideas but reducing the number of words. Try to use no more than 70 words.

> It was a law firm that was probably the only one of its kind in existence. One of the attorneys was rather heavy of body; the other was awkwardly tall and thin. Both believed in being thoroughly open and honest in expressing what they thought. Both, therefore, had little patience with individuals who were in the habit of making an appearance of importance or dignity. Occasionally, the two of them disagreed, but they never quarreled over petty things. Both always felt pity for the unfortunate, and they would try to do all they could to alleviate their grief and anxiety. It is no wonder, then, that the people who engaged their professional services did so with a feeling of trust.

GENERAL INDEX

VOCABULARY INDEX

passionately, 191
patient, 45
patron, 177
pause, 101
perceive, 158
perplex, 30
persevere, 191
persist, 191
pious, 156
placid, 45
plague, 205
plea, 217
pompous, 177
portly, 178
positively, 87
practically, 18
precepts, 156
precipitate, 73
prevail, 75
pride, 18
prior, 144
projectile, 31
prompt, 75
prophetic, 75
prospective, 18
provoke, 75
prowl, 133
prudence, 156

quarry, 100

rage, 118
ragged, 177
rake, 28
rash, 7
rawboned, 204
reckless, 7, 205
recurrence, 145
refuge, 7
reliance, 217
relinquish, 205
rend, 45
repent, 75
resentment, 6
resist, 119
restrain, 132
reticence, 218
reveal, 191
rigid, 101
root, 9
ruse, 158

scrub, 132
sensation, 205
sensitive, 101
sequence, 64
series, 64
shaggy, 31
shoo, 45
shuffle, 64
shyly, 218

significance, 191
sluggishly, 6
soar, 192
soberly, 64
solace, 157, 205
solitary, 64
sorties, 28
sparse, 30
squabble, 191
squirm, 119
stratagem, 158
stress, 101
stupefy, 87
submission, 119
submit, 119
succession, 64
suspiciously, 45
sustained, 156
sympathize, 205

tactfully, 45
tattered, 87
tautness, 101
tension, 101
terrified, 87
terror, 87
testimonial, 156
tilt, 145
timidly, 218
titter, 7

torment, 205
transform, 157
traverse, 192

undemonstrative, 74
unique, 178
unity, 186
unparalleled, 178
unremarkable, 177

vacant, 7
valiantly, 218
vehement, 45
vex, 205
vision, 101
voluntary, 218

wary, 7
wheedle, 44
whimper, 133
whine, 102, 133
withdraw, 87
wither, 191
wrangle, 191
writhe, 119

yield, 119

zeal, 119